TWO HUNDRED MODERN CHESS TRAPS
IN THE FIANCHETTO OPENINGS

J. B. HOWSON

Two Hundred Modern Chess Traps in the Fianchetto openings

SOUTH BRUNSWICK AND NEW YORK

A. S. BARNES AND COMPANY

First American edition published 1971 by
A. S. Barnes and Co. Inc., Cranbury, New Jersey 08512

Library of Congress Catalogue Card Number: 77-151123

ISBN 0-498-07919-8

PRINTED IN THE UNITED STATES OF AMERICA

FOREWORD

Fianchetto chess is here to stay! With the tremendous advance in "hypermodern" theory during recent years, no player wishing to hold his own in competitive play can afford to ignore the new techniques which are now available.

In assembling these 200 traps, the author has made a deep study of systems used by four original thinkers of the present day—Tal, Fischer, Larsen and Penrose. Sparks can normally be expected to fly when players like these sit down at the board, and new pitfalls for the unwary are constantly being revealed in their games.

One typical instance is the strategical error which cost Tal his game against Penrose in the 1960 Chess Olympics at Leipzig (and which incidentally was the only game lost by any Soviet player in the whole tournament!). This sensational encounter, involving the first defeat of a reigning world champion in the 20th century by a Briton, is analysed in the chapter on the Modern Benoni Defence.

This book is designed to help the average player chart a safe course through the shoals which abound in each fianchetto opening. Every endeavour has been made to restrict the traps given to those discovered during the last two decades—except in cases where a really important line dates back earlier —and the original source is recorded where it seems conclusive that the pitfall in question claimed its first victim in one particular game.

However, the question of "first ever" is a notoriously difficult one, so apologies are made in advance to aggrieved parties who may find their own pet winning device (which may have given them good service since the year dot) credited to some grandmaster or other at a later date.

The author hopes to make readers familiar with the *types* of trap characteristic of fianchetto play, not just with specific variations. Very often a player can sense the possibility of a hidden snare if the type of position involved is well known to him.

In addition, the book can be used to develop tactical ability. Just cover the PLAY NOW CONTINUED text below each diagram, and try to work out just why the last move was a mistake. Choose a line of your own, and see how near you can get to the correct refutation before reading on.

CONTENTS

Position after 11 P–B3?

THE OPENING MOVES WERE:

The prize for the most successful trap of recent times must surely go to Soviet grandmaster Geller, for his win against the Polish master Adamski, in round 9 of the 1968 Olympics Finals at Lugano, and his win two rounds later *with exactly the same variation* against the Danish player Holm! This featured a theme peculiar to the King's Indian Defence, where Black's King's Knight is sacrificed on K5.

	Adamski Holm	Geller
1	P–Q4	N–KB3
2	P–QB4	P–KN3
3	N–QB3	B–N2
4	P–K4	P–Q3
5	B–K2	O–O
6	B–N5	

Designed to put pressure on Black's KR3 straight away by Q–Q2, etc.

6	...	QN–Q2
7	Q–Q2	P–K4
8	N–B3	P–B3
9	O–O	PxP

Tal has shown the right way here, in his game against **Borisenko**, Spartakiade 1967, which continued 9 ... Q–R4, 10 KR–Q1 R–K1, 11 P–Q5 PxP, 12 NxQP QxQ, 13 NxN ch BxN, 14 RxQ BxB, 15 NxB P–B3 with equality.

10	NxP	N–B4
11	P–B3?	

White should instead make the best of a bad job by moving his Queen again, to QB2.

PLAY NOW CONTINUED:

11	...	KNxP!

and Black either wins a pawn or gets an overwhelming position.

For example, Adamski-Geller continued 12 NxN NxN, 13 PxN BxN ch, 14 QxB QxB, 15 QxQP Q–K6 ch, 16 R–B2 B–K3, 17 QB4 QxQ, 18 RxQ QR–Q1, etc.

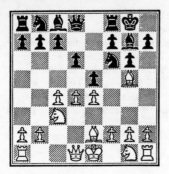

Position after 6 ... P–K4??

THE OPENING MOVES WERE:

White	Black
1 P–Q4	N–KB3
2 P–QB4	P–KN3
3 N–QB3	B–N2
4 P–K4	P–Q3
5 B–K2	O–O
6 B–N5	
6 ...	P–K4??

PLAY NOW CONTINUES:

	White	Black
7	PxP!	PxP
8	QxQ	RxQ
9	BxN	BxB
10	N–Q5!	

People have got so used to playing an "automatic" ... P–K4 in the orthodox 5 B–K2 (or 5 N–B3 and 6 B–K2) line that it is worth pointing out that this immediate advance is not sound against *every* White system. In the top diagram, Black has sleepily continued with his usual ... P–K4, thinking that White's previous move makes no difference one way or the other. A rude awakening awaits him ...

This system, popularised by the Soviet player Averbakh, must be handled with great care by Black.

A good sixth move for him is given on the facing page.

and Black must lose at least the exchange.

Position after 8 N–KB3?

PLAY NOW CONTINUES:

8 ...	P–N4!
9 PxP	PxP
10 Q–B2	

Probably the best sixth move of all for Black is 6 ... P–B4, which sets in motion an immediate counter attack against the Queen's side weakened by the absence of White's QB. White has little option but to reply 7 P–Q5 (7 PxP? is answered by ... Q–R4!, threatening 8 ... NxKP), and the game can continue 7 ... P–QR3, 8 P–QR4! Q–R4, etc. If White omits the important advance of the QRP, and plays a developing move instead (say, 8 N–KB3?), he soon gets into hot water.

10 BxP permits the neat riposte ... NxKP!, 11 NxN Q–R4 ch, etc., with advantage to Black.

10 ...	P–N5
11 N–Q1	P–N6!
12 QxNP	NxKP
13 O–O	NxB
14 NxN	P–K4!

with a fine game for Black.

Here, in contrast to the Adamski/Holm-Geller variation, Black gets into hot water through playing . . . KNxKP. This particular line of the King's Indian (8 . . . R–K1 and 9 . . . PxP) offers Black very little choice of moves until well into the middlegame, so masters who like to get moving early on usually play 8 . . . P–B3 and 9 . . . Q–R4 or N3 instead. Tal, for example, has had much success with both these lines.

Position after 12 . . . KNxP?

THE OPENING MOVES WERE:

	White	Black
1	P–Q4	N–KB3
2	P–QB4	P–KN3
3	P–KN3	B–N2
4	B–N2	O–O
5	N–KB3	P–Q3
6	O–O	QN–Q2
7	N–B3	P–K4
8	P–K4	R–K1

Black starts to line up his pieces on the White KP, before pushing forward on the Queen's side with . . . P–QR4–R5, etc.

9	P–KR3	PxP
10	NxP	N–B4
11	R–K1	P–QR4
12	Q–B2	

Protecting the KP once again so that he can continue with 13 B–K3 and 14 QR–Q1. Inexperienced players, spotting the unsupported N on Q4, often think this move is a blunder, and continue with . . .

12 . . .		KNxP?

The correct move, 12 . . . P–R5, is discussed on the following page.

PLAY NOW CONTINUES:

13	NxN	BxN
14	B–N5!	Q–Q2
15	N–B6 ch	BxN
16	BxB	

14 . . . P–B3? loses to 15 BxP BxB, 16 NxB ch QxQ, 17 RxR ch.

and Black's King's position has been fatally weakened.

4

Position after 16 RxP?

On the preceding page, we saw Black making the mistake of grabbing a pawn on the 12th move, when White appeared to have blundered with 12 Q–B2. Black's correct move (or at least, a very good one) is 12 . . . P–R5. In this variation, paradoxically, Black in turn can offer a "poison pawn" if White selects the continuation 15 N(4)–K2. If this Greek gift is accepted, White soon gets into grave difficulties, as shown below.

THE OPENING MOVES WERE:

	Euwe	Najdorf
	(Leipzig, 1960)	
1	P–Q4	N–KB3
2	P–QB4	P–KN3
3	P–KN3	B–N2
4	B–N2	O–O
5	N–KB3	P–Q3
6	O–O	QN–Q2
7	N–B3	P–K4
8	P–K4	R–K1
9	P–KR3	PxP
10	NxP	N–B4
11	R–K1	P–QR4
12	Q–B2	P–R5
13	B–K3	P–B3
14	QR–Q1	KN–Q2
15	N(4)–K2	

15 P–B4 is probably the best move here, so as to create chances for White on the King's side.

15	. . .	Q–R4
16	RxP?	

Euwe-Najdorf continued 16 N–N1 N–K4, 17 R–KB1 Q–N5, 18 N–R3 P–B4, 19 PxP BxP, 20 Q–Q2 etc.

PLAY NOW CONTINUES:

16	. . .	N–K4!
17	P–N3	PxP
18	PxP	BxP!

and White is struggling.

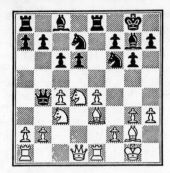

Position after 12 ... Q–N5?

If Black selects the sharp 9 ... Q–R4 variation, he must be very careful not to plunge his Queen into hot water by chasing after White's QBP at the wrong moment. (However, properly handled, this early sortie by the Black Queen can pose difficult problems for White, as is demonstrated in the lower half of the page).

THE OPENING MOVES WERE:

Kotov (Riga, 1958)	Tal
1 P–Q4	N–KB3
2 P–QB4	P–KN3
3 P–KN3	B–N2
4 B–N2	O–O
5 N–KB3	P–Q3
6 O–O	QN–Q2
7 N–B3	P–K4
8 P–K4	P–B3
9 P–KR3	Q–R4
10 R–K1	

Reasonable alternatives here are: B–K3, Q–B2, P–Q5 and PxP.

10 ...	PxP

This is where we part company with the Kotov-Tal game, which continued: 10 ... R–K1, 11 P–QR3 PxP, 12 NxP N–K4, 13 B–KB1 P–QR3, 14 B–Q2? Q–N3, 15 B–K3 P–QB4, 16 N–N3 B–K3, 17 N–Q2 N–QB3 with advantage to Black. The text continuation is **Vladimirov-Savon**, Baku 1961.

11 NxP	R–K1
12 B–K3	Q–N5?

PLAY NOW CONTINUED:

13 P–QR3!	Q–R4

13 ... QxBP?? would be very poor here, because of 14 B–KB1 Q–B4, 15 N–B5!, etc.—and of course 13 ... QxNP?? loses to 14 N–QR4!, etc.

14 P–QN4	Q–B2
15 R–QB1	P–QR4
16 P–B4	

with a big positional plus for White.

Position after 17 PxP?

PLAY NOW CONTINUES:

White	Black
17 ...	BxQBP!
18 RxR ch	NxR
19 BxB	P–Q4
20 B–B4	Q–N3

A much better overall plan for Black is 11 ... N–K4!, 12 B–B1 R–K1, 13 R–N1 B–K3, 14 P–QN4 Q–B2, 15 P–B4 N(4)–Q2. If White now makes the mistake of rushing forward on the King's side, he can get into a mess, as shown in the accompanying diagram after 16 P–KB5 PxP, 17 PxP?. Good strategy for both sides was featured in the game **Smyslov-Stein**, Moscow 1967, which continued: 16 B–K3 P–QR4, 17 P–N5 N–B4, 18 NxB NxN, 19 Q–B3 N–Q2 =.

and Black will soon regain his piece with a slight advantage.

7

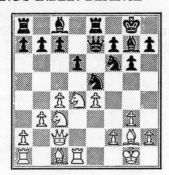

Position after 12 P–N3?

The weakness on KB3, which caused White's downfall on page 5, can also arise when Q–B2 and R–Q1 have been played in an attempt to discourage ... P–QB3. In the game discussed here, White fails to take advantage of the badly placed Black Queen on K2, and is swept away in a maelstrom of complications.

THE OPENING MOVES WERE:

Keene　　**Wright**
(Bognor Regis training tournament, 1967)

	Keene	Wright
1	P–Q4	N–KB3
2	N–KB3	P–KN3
3	P–KN3	B–N2
4	B–N2	O–O
5	O–O	P–Q3
6	P–B4	QN–Q2
7	Q–B2	P–K4
8	R–Q1	R–K1
9	N–B3	Q–K2!?

With idea of playing the QN to K4, but leaving himself open to the reply N–Q5 at some stage.

10	P–K4	PxP
11	NxP	N–K4
12	P–N3?	

Fatally weakening the long diagonal. 12 N–Q5! is much better.

PLAY NOW CONTINUED:

12	...	B–N5!
13	R–KB1	

13 P–B3 would have been answered by ... P–B4!, etc.

13	...	P–QB4
14	N(4)–K2	N–B6 ch
15	K–R1	NxKP
16	N–Q5	Q–K4
17	B–B4??	

A horrible blunder in a lost position.

17	...	QxR!
18	Resigns	

since the other Rook cannot leave the KBP unguarded to capture the Queen.

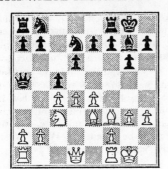

The defensive manoeuvre . . . KN–Q2 often comes in very handy as a method of bringing pressure to bear along the diagonal, and supporting the advance . . . P–QB4. However, it can be overdone, as in the diagrammed position, where Black has carried out the plan with his QN still sitting at home. This game was played at Kecskemet, 1968.

Position after 11 . . . P–QB4?

THE OPENING MOVES WERE:

	Lengyel	Honfi
1	P–Q4	N–KB3
2	P–QB4	P–KN3
3	P–KN3	B–N2
4	B–N2	O–O
5	N–QB3	P–Q3
6	N–KB3	P–QB3

(**Keene-Penrose,** London, 1967, went: 6 . . . QN–Q2, 7 Q–B2 P–B3, 8 O–O Q–B2, 9 P–N3 P–QN4, 10 N–Q2 B–N2, 11 B–N2 QR–B1, 12 QR–B1 P–QR3, 13 P–K3 Q–N1, 14 KR–Q1 KR–Q1, 15 Q–N1 P–K3, 16 QN–K4! with some advantage to White.)

7	O–O	Q–R4
8	P–K4	B–KN5
9	P–KR3	BxN
10	BxB	KN–Q2!?
11	B–K3	P–QB4?

PLAY NOW CONTINUED:

12	PxP	NxP
13	P–K5!	N–QB3
14	PxP	KR–Q1
15	N–Q5!	P–K3
16	N–B7	QR–QB1
17	P–QR3!	BxP
18	R–QN1	N–R5

but this also left him with a lost game after 19 B–Q2 N–B6, 20 KBxN! RxP, 21 BxN QxN, 22 Q–B3! so that if BxB, 23 BxP R–QN1, 24 P–B5 QxP, 25 KR–QB1 etc.

9

In the 6 ... N–QB3 line, if White castles at the seventh turn Black can bring his QB to KB4 at once, hoping for a chance to get his KN onto K5. A good counter to this is 8 N–K1!, followed by 9 P–Q5. Black's QN will normally go to his usual post on QR4, to aid in the coming Queen's side push. Naturally the Knight is out on a limb here, and due care must be taken that White doesn't simply "snap the branch off".

Position after 15 ... P–QR3??

THE OPENING MOVES WERE:

Portisch	Tal
(Moscow, 1967)	
1 N–KB3	N–KB3
2 P–QB4	P–KN3
3 P–Q4	B–N2
4 P–KN3	O–O
5 B–N2	P–Q3
6 N–QB3	N–QB3
7 O–O	B–KB4
8 N–K1	P–K4

8 ... Q–Q2? is discussed lower down the page.

9 P–Q5	N–QR4
10 P–K4	B–KN5
11 Q–Q3	P–QB4

Stopping P–QN4, which would trap the wandering Knight.

12 B–Q2	N–KR4
13 N–B2	B–Q2?

Intent upon his aggressive plans for King's side expansion, Tal omits the essential defensive preliminary ... P–QN3.

14 N–N5!	BxN
15 PxB	P–QR3??

But this makes things a thousand times worse than they were already. The unpalatable ... P–QN3 was an absolute must here.

PLAY NOW CONTINUED:

16 P–N6!	QxP
17 Q–QB3	

and the Knight is lost.

At Leningrad, 1967, in the game **Korchnoi-Westerinen,** Black chose the inferior eighth move . . . Q–Q2?, which leaves White with virtually a free hand in the centre.

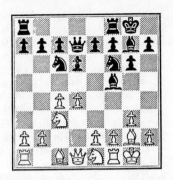

Position after 8 . . . Q–Q2?

PLAY NOW CONTINUED:

	White	Black
9	P–Q5	N–QR4
10	P–K4	B–R6
11	Q–K2	P–QB4
12	P–KB4!	

and Westerinen found himself wishing he had played . . . P–K4 instead of . . . Q–Q2, since he could not now prevent the crushing P–K5.

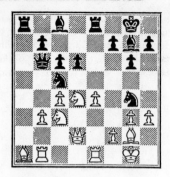

Position after 17 P–R3?

At one time it was thought that the best place for White's QB was QN2, to confront the Bishop on Black's KN2. This was before it was realised that Black could afford to weaken his QP with . . . P–QB3 in order to venture forth on the Queen's side with . . . Q–N3 or . . . Q–R4, hitting at the weak Black squares on that side of the board. The turning point for the whole variation came when Bronstein slaughtered Zita in the 1946 Moscow vs Prague match. It is difficult to pinpoint an actual outright blunder in White's opening play, so I have chosen instead to diagram the critical point of the early middlegame.

THE OPENING MOVES WERE:

	Zita	Bronstein
1	P–QB4	P–K4
2	N–QB3	N–KB3
3	N–B3	P–Q3
4	P–Q4	QN–Q2
5	P–KN3	P–KN3
6	B–N2	B–N2
7	O–O	O–O
8	P–N3	R–K1
9	B–N2	P–B3
10	P–K4	PxP
11	NxP	Q–N3
12	Q–Q2	N–B4
13	KR–K1	P–QR4
14	QR–N1	

Most modern masters would have played P–KR3 by now, in order to guard against . . . N–KN5 by Black at an awkward moment.

14	. . .	P–R5
15	B–QR1	PxP
16	PxP	N–N5
17	P–R3?	

Failing to appreciate Black's evil plans.

PLAY NOW CONTINUED:

17	. . .	RxB!
18	RxR	NxBP!

and White's position is shattered.

The game continued 19 R–K3 (if 19 QxN N–Q6!, and if 19 KxN NxNP!) NxRP ch, 20 K–R2 N–B7, 21 R–B3 QNxKP, 22 Q–B4 N–N5 ch, 23 K–R1 P–KB4, 24 NxN RxN, 25 QxQP RxN, and White resigned on the 31st move.

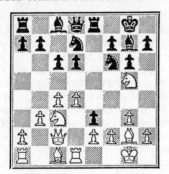

Position after 12 BxP?

THE OPENING MOVES WERE:

	White	Black
1	P–Q4	N–KB3
2	P–QB4	P–KN3
3	P–KN3	B–N2
4	B–N2	O–O
5	N–KB3	P–Q3
6	O–O	QN–Q2
7	N–B3	P–K4
8	P–N3	
8	...	R–K1
9	Q–B2	P–B3
10	R–Q1	P–K5
11	N–KN5	
11	...	P–K6!
12	BxP?	

PLAY NOW CONTINUES:

12	...	RxB!
13	PxR	N–N5

Special problems arise for both sides when White omits the usual P–K4 in the Fianchetto variation, and tries instead to upset Black with an early R–Q1. Black has no advanced KP to press down on, and must look for alternative counter-play. One method is to rush his KP forward on to the fifth rank as soon as the White Rook reaches Q1. Very tricky play can then take place on the King's file, particularly if Black is able to push the KP even further on to the sixth rank.

This, or Q–B2, is normally the signal that White is going to try R–Q1.

The other way of putting pressure on the KP, 11 N–Q2, can be answered by ... P–Q4, 12 PxP PxP, 13 N–N5 R–K3, 14 Q–B7 Q–K1, 15 B–QR3 B–B1 with equality.

regaining the exchange with much the better position.

White's correct continuation is 12 PxP!, as in **Donner–Szabo**, 1956, but Black regains his pawn eventually with an equal game: 12 ... N–B1, 13 P–K4 Q–K2, 14 P–K3 B–KR3!, 15 N–B3 NxP, 16 NxN QxN, 17 QxQ RxQ, etc.

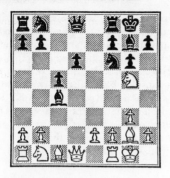

Position after 9 ... BxP?

THE OPENING MOVES WERE:

One of the most interesting recent developments in the 6 ... P–QB4 Yugoslav variation is an exchange sacrifice by Black, arising from the line 7 ... P–K3. This has been found to be so strong over the board that a method has been worked out by means of which White can avoid the possibility altogether *without* making any radical alteration to his general plan in the opening. Prospective adherents of the Yugoslav must learn to recognise the "avoidance play" even when somewhat obscured by transposition.

	Korchnoi	Bouaziz
	(Sousse, 1967)	
1	P–Q4	N–KB3
2	P–QB4	P–KN3
3	P–KN3	B–N2
4	B–N2	O–O
5	N–KB3	P–Q3
6	O–O!	

This is the "avoidance play", designed to invalidate the exchange sacrifice discussed in the lower half of the page.

(It can also be disguised by a crafty transposition, as in the game **Keene-Wibe**, Jerusalem, 1967; which went: 5 N–KB3 P–B4, 6 P–Q5 P–Q3, 7 O–O P–K3, 8 PxP BxP, 9 N–N5 N–B3!—*not* falling into the trap by 9 ... BxP?, etc. Nevertheless, White's position here seems superior after 10 NxB PxN, 11 N–B3, since Black's solid centre is not quite sufficient compensation for White's Bishop pair.)

6	...	P–B4
7	P–Q5	P–K3
8	PxP	BxP
9	N–N5	BxP?

Korchnoi-Bouaziz continued:

PLAY NOW CONTINUED:

10	BxP	QN–Q2
11	N–R3!	N–N3

Korchnoi-Velimirovic, USSR vs Yugoslavia, 1966, went 11 ... R–N1, 12 NxB RxB, 13 NxP with a won game for White.

12	NxB	NxN
13	BxR	QxB

and Black has nothing for the exchange.

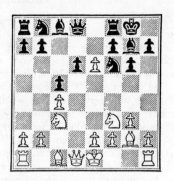

Position after 8 PxP?

The first five moves are the same as Korchnoi-Bouaziz, and then White plays 6 N–B3 P–B4, 7 P–Q5 P–K3, 8 PxP? There seems little doubt now that this move deserves a question mark— White's best here appears to be 8 O–O, transposing into the Modern Benoni.

PLAY NOW CONTINUES:

	White	Black
8	...	BxP
9	N–N5	BxP
10	BxP	QN–Q2
11	BxR	QxB
12	O–O	P–Q4

with a very fine position indeed.

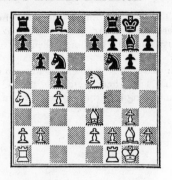

Position after 12 N–K5?

One drawback of the otherwise promising Yugoslav system is that White can, without risk of losing the initiative, force the Queens off and create a symmetrical position after eight or nine moves *with White to move*. Black must soon stop copying moves—whether he has been doing so consciously or unconsciously—or White will simply gain control of the open Queen's file. The theme of the two traps on this page is that White must not imagine however that his pressure on the long diagonal will win the game of its own accord.

THE OPENING MOVES WERE:

	White	Black
1	P–Q4	N–KB3
2	P–QB4	P–KN3
3	P–KN3	B–N2
4	B–N2	O–O
5	N–KB3	P–Q3
6	O–O	

(The game **Lengyel-Penrose,** Enschede, 1963, went: 6 N–B3 P–B4, 7 PxP PxP, 8 QxQ RxQ, 9 B–K3 N–B3, 10 BxP B–K3, 11 N–Q2 N–Q2, 12 B–QR3 N–N3, 13 BxN PxB, 14 BxP R–K1, 15 B–B5 NxP, 16 O–O–O and Black hadn't really got enough for his pawn.)

6	...	P–B4
7	N–B3	N–B3
8	PxP	PxP
9	B–K3	Q–R4!

Now White ought to be thinking on tactical lines. For example, a reasonable plan is to move the Bishop again (!), as in **Pachman-Fischer,** Havana, 1965: 10 B–Q2! B–B4, 11 Q–B1 N–Q5, 12 NxN PxN, 13 N–Q5 Q–Q1, 14 B–R6+.

10	Q–R4?	QxQ
11	NxQ	P–N3!
12	N–K5??	

Daring White to take action on the diagonal. If he does . . .

PLAY NOW CONTINUES:

12	...	NxN!
13	BxR	B–Q2

and White has two pieces and a pawn en prise.

Position after 13 N–K5?

PLAY THEN CONTINUES:

The same trap exists in a slightly different form on the next move, if White chooses the more sensible 12 QR–Q1, but then yields after all to the temptation of N–K5 when Black replies ... B–N2.

13 ...	NxN
14 BxB	NxP!
15 BxR	NxB
16 PxN	RxB

with more than enough positional compensation for the exchange.

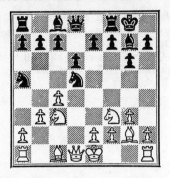

Position after 8 . . . NxQP??

If Black selects a Yugoslav type set-up, by placing his QN on QB3 and then moving it to QR4 after White pushes forward with P–Q5, the White Queen's side comes under a lot of pressure at an early stage in the game. The pawn move P–QN3 is an obvious and sound method of bolstering up the pawn centre. The consequent temporary weakness on the long diagonal cannot be exploited, as play from the diagrammed position shows. This first trap is a sideline from the game Donner-Penrose, Holland vs England, 1966, which is further examined lower down the page.

THE OPENING MOVES WERE:

	Donner	Penrose
1	P–Q4	N–KB3
2	P–QB4	P–KN3
3	P–KN3	B–N2
4	B–N2	O–O
5	N–QB3	P–Q3
6	N–B3	N–B3

This move is the signal that Black is prepared to concentrate his attentions on the Queen's wing, if White takes up the challenge by P–Q5.

| 7 | P–Q5 | |

The alternative plan of doing nothing in particular (by 7 O–O and 8 P–KR3, etc.) can be effectively countered by the Panno System of . . . P–QR3, . . . R–QN1 and . . . P–QN4.

| 7 | . . . | N–QR4 |
| 8 | P–N3 | NxQP?? |

PLAY WOULD NOW CONTINUE:

9	NxN!	BxR
10	B–Q2	NxQBP
11	PxN	B–N2
12	O–O	

and White's two Knights will be much stronger in the middlegame than Black's Rook and two pawns.

(Penrose actually played 8 . . . P–B4, and the game was eventually drawn. It is worth looking through the next few moves, to see how the players set about their respective tasks in the strategical sense: 9 B–N2 P–QR3, 10 O–O R–N1, 11 N–Q2 P–QN4, 12 Q–B2 P–K4, 13 PxP ep PxP, and the stage was set for an interesting struggle.)

Position after 9 B–Q2?

Once having embarked upon one of the stereotyped lines, such as Petrosian's 7 P–Q5, White must usually adhere rigidly to thematic play for the next few moves if he wishes to retain the initiative. In the diagrammed position, White has chosen 9 B–Q2? rather than the normal 9 B–R4 P–KN4, 10 B–N3 N–R4, doubtless hoping to launch a pawn attack on the King's side without having to allow the exchange of his QB. Retribution comes swiftly . . .

THE OPENING MOVES WERE:

Milan	Wills
(British Correspondence Championship 1968/69)	
1 P–Q4	N–KB3
2 P–QB4	P–KN3
3 N–QB3	B–N2
4 P–K4	P–Q3
5 N–KB3	O–O
6 B–K2	P–K4
7 P–Q5	QN–Q2

7 . . . N–R3 is a good alternative which usually transposes into . . . QN–Q2 line, and has the advantage of keeping the line of Black's QB open. However, one little-known drawback with this method was demonstrated in the game **Adaway–Penrose**, 1968, when White continued 8 N–Q2?!, and Black found himself unable to prepare the way for a thematic . . . N–QB4 because his own Knight prevented the "natural" advance . . . P–QR4. Penrose eventually won the game though.

8 B–KN5	P–KR3
9 B–Q2?	

PLAY NOW CONTINUED:

9 . . .	N–B4
10 Q–B2	KNxKP!
11 NxN	B–B4
12 B–Q3	BxN
13 BxB	P–KB4

and Black regained his piece with advantage.

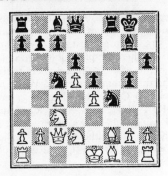

Position after 16 KBPxP?

When Black counteracts the Petrosian System with ... P–KR3 and ... P–KN4, followed by ... N–KR4, White has the choice of the sharp 11 P–KR4 or the positional 11 N–Q2. In the latter line, the Black Knight must of course go immediately to B5 to get out of the line of fire of White's KB. At this point White can be tempted to preserve his Bishop pair at the expense of common-sense play. The diagrammed position arose during the 1964 Buenos Aires tournament.

THE OPENING MOVES WERE:

	Najdorf	R. Byrne
1	P–Q4	N–KB3
2	P–QB4	P–KN3
3	N–QB3	B–N2
4	P–K4	P–Q3
5	N–B3	O–O
6	B–K2	P–K4
7	P–Q5	QN–Q2
8	B–N5	P–KR3
9	B–R4	P–KN4
10	B–N3	N–R4
11	N–Q2	N–B5
12	B–B1!?	N–B4

It is worth noting here that if White had selected the sound 12 O–O instead, then 13 B–N4? here would be countered by the familiar thematic stroke ... NxKP!, 14 NxN P–KB4, etc.

13	Q–B2	P–B4
14	P–B3!?	P–B3
15	B–B2	KBPxP
16	KBPxP?	

16 N(2)xP was essential.

PLAY SHOULD NOW HAVE CONTINUED:

16 ... N(4)–Q6 ch!, 17 BxN NxP ch, and White would have had to humbly play 18 K–Q1 (18 K–B1 loses the Queen to ... N–K6 ch, and 18 K–K2 fails against ... B–N5 ch). However, Byrne missed the combination! He played 16 ... PxP instead—but eventually won anyway.

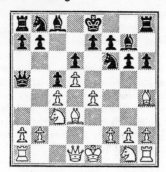

Where White tries a very early B–KN5, it is usually best for Black to play an immediate . . . P–KR3 to stop a possible Q–Q2 and B–KR6, and then to strike back at once in the centre with the thematic . . . P–QB4. In the diagrammed position, White has locked the centre with P–Q5, but failed to relieve the pin on his QN. This game was played in the USSR Teams Tournament, 1966.

Position after 8 B–Q3?

THE OPENING MOVES WERE:

	Stein	Geller
1	P–Q4	N–KB3
2	P–QB4	P–KN3
3	N–QB3	B–N2
4	P–K4	P–Q3
5	B–N5	

(If 4 N–KB3 is substituted for P–K4 in this line, then Black has available the manoeuvre 5 . . . P–KR3, 6 B–R4 P–KN4, 7 B–N3 N–R4!, since the White Queen is not guarding that square. This variation was featured in the first game of the 1958 British Championship play-off, between **Penrose** and **Barden,** which continued 8 P–K3 P–QB3, 9 B–Q3 N–Q2, 10 Q–B2 N–N3, with equality.)

5 . . .	P–KR3
6 B–R4	P–QB4!

(Black must keep the pressure up. Both 6 . . . P–B3 and 6 . . . O–O would be met by 7 P–B4! Failure to advance the KBP at this stage gives Black the chance to equalise—i.e. 6 . . . O–O, 7 Q–Q2? P–KN4, 8 B–N3 N–R4, 9 O–O–O QN–B3, 10 P–Q5 N–Q5, 11 P–B3 P–K4 =, as in **Tal–Hort,** Prague, 1961.)

7 P–Q5	Q–R4
8 B–Q3?	Best is 8 Q–Q2.

PLAY NOW CONTINUED:

8 . . .	NxKP!
9 BxN	BxN ch
10 PxB	QxP ch
11 K–B1	P–KN4!
12 B–N3	P–B4

Now Black is going to get his piece back, and there seems no way in which White can restore the material balance while he is doing it.

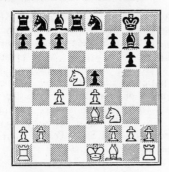

Position after 9 . . . N–K1?

THE OPENING MOVES WERE:

The idea of moving the QB to K3 before developing the KB has become known as the Larsen Attack, due principally to its use by the Danish grandmaster during his great run of tournament successes in 1967. The theorists are not yet agreed upon what constitutes Black's best line of defence. In the top diagram, we have the position resulting from Miagmasuren's faulty ninth move at Sousse, 1967.

	Larsen	Miagmasuren
1	P–QB4	N–KB3
2	N–KB3	P–KN3
3	N–B3	B–N2
4	P–K4	P–Q3
5	P–Q4	O–O
6	B–K3	P–K4
7	PxP	PxP
8	QxQ	RxQ
9	N–Q5	N–K1?

6 . . . QN–Q2 is less committal for Black, and may be best here.

The net result of this move is that White has achieved a very good variation of the Exchange System, with his QB actively placed on K3 instead of the KB passively placed on K2.

PLAY NOW CONTINUED:

10	O–O–O	R–Q2
11	B–K2	P–QB3
12	N–B3	P–B3
13	P–B5	

and Black was slowly strangled to death in 38 moves.

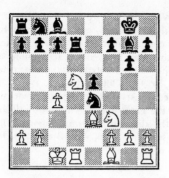

Position after 10 ... NxP?

PLAY WOULD NOW CONTINUE:

11 NxBP!!	RxN
12 R–Q8 ch	B–B1
13 B–R6	N–Q2
14 NxP	

KING'S INDIAN DEFENCE

Black has two reasonable alternatives at move 9, the first being to take the Knight off and then hit the resulting pawn on Q5 straight away. This line was played in the **Larsen-Toran** game at Palma, 1967: 9 ... NxN, 10 BPxN P–QB3, 11 B–QB4 P–QN4, 12 B–N3 B–N2, 13 R–QB1 P–KR3, 14 O–O P–QR4, 15 PxP BxP, 16 R–B5 P–R5, and White had only a slight advantage. The second possibility is 9 ... R–Q2!, 10 O–O–O (10 NxKP? loses material after ... NxN, 11 NxR NxB, etc.). Now 10 ... NxP? is very tempting ...

and Black will surely never emerge alive, whichever move he now chooses to stave off immediate mate.

Black can hold the position at the tenth move, though, as was demonstrated in the 1968 **Tal-Gligoric** match, when play continued 10 ... N–B3, 11 B–Q3 N–KN5!=.

23

Position after 11 ... P–Q4?

THE OPENING MOVES WERE:

Where White proceeds quietly on "orthodox" lines, and then holds back the committal move P–Q5 in favour of further development, Black's main aim in life will be to explode the centre with ... PxQP followed by ... P–Q4. But Black must make proper preparations for the great event. The position shown in the diagram is from Gligoric-Pilnik, Amsterdam, 1950, with Black launching out too soon.

	Gligoric	Pilnik
1	P–Q4	N–KB3
2	P–QB4	P–KN3
3	N–QB3	B–N2
4	P–K4	P–Q3
5	N–B3	O–O
6	B–K2	P–K4
7	O–O	QN–Q2
8	R–K1	P–B3
9	B–KB1	

White must not switch suddenly to the "Petrosian plan" P–Q5 now (as indeed did **Petrosian** himself against **Spassky** in the 1960 USSR Championship!), because his eighth move will then be revealed as pointless.

The cautious 9 ... R–K1 is best here.

9	...	PxP?
10	NxP	R–K1
11	B–B4	P–Q4?

Doubtless carried away by the prospect of being able to play the "beautiful" 12 ... NxQP, Pilnik overlooks the simple fact that his opponent may not mind having to reply 13 PxN.

PLAY NOW CONTINUED:

12	BPxP	NxQP!?
13	PxN	RxR
14	QxR	BxN
15	R–Q1!	

and Black is left floundering in the ruins of his own combination—i.e., after 15 ... B–N2, 16 PxP PxP, 17 B–B4 Pilnik found himself with virtually a lost game.

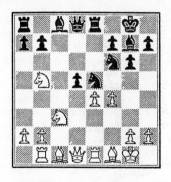

Position after 14 P-KB4??

In the game **Koblentz-A. Geller,** Riga, 1962, Black again ventured the dubious 11 ... P–Q4: (e.g., after 9 ... R–K1, 10 R–QN1 PxP, 11 NxP). But this time fortune favoured the brave, and White allowed himself the luxury of just one prod too many before picking up the proferred QP: 12 BPxP PxP, 13 N(4)–N5! N–K4, 14 P–KB4?? (the mercenary 14 PxP is perfectly OK here).

PLAY NOW CONTINUED:

14 ...	N(3)–KN5!!
15 R–K2	

something had to be done to try and alleviate the effect of that horrible check which is coming on QN6.

15 ...	Q–N3 ch
12 K–R1	N–QB3
17 N–Q6	N–Q5
18 NxB	NxR!
19 QxN	N–B7 ch
20 Resigns	

since mate or loss of Queen is inevitable.

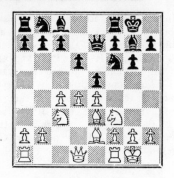

Position after 8 O–O?

THE OPENING MOVES WERE:

	Stein	Gufeld
	(Tiflis, 1967)	
1	P–Q4	N–KB3
2	P–QB4	P–KN3
3	N–QB3	B–N2
4	P–K4	P–Q3
5	N–B3	O–O
6	B–K2	P–K4
7	B–K3	

7 ...		Q–K2!?
8 O–O?		

PLAY NOW CONTINUES:

8 ...	NxKP!
9 NxN	PxP
10 KNxP	QxN

The Yugoslav grandmaster Gligoric has tried to infuse more life into White's play, in the B–K2 line, by bringing his QB to K3 on the seventh move instead of castling (see page 22 for Larsen's similar attempt with 6 B–K3). The idea is to gain a tempo for the central or Queen's side attack if Black incautiously chooses the wrong reply—such as he has done in the top diagram, with 7 ... Q–K2!? But White must also play accurately ...

Black has several good moves here, the ones that *aren't* good being ... Q–K2!? and ... N–B3? In both cases White can reply 8 P–Q5, either rendering the Queen move pointless, or driving the Knight back before Black knows for sure where to put it.

But this is the very move which Black was hoping for in playing the Queen to K2!

That theme crops up once again!

and White's centre and Queen's side is considerably weakened by the lonely QBP stranded on the fourth rank.

Better play for White was featured in the game **Gligoric-Fischer,** Monaco, 1967, which went: 8 P–Q5! N–K1, 9 P–KR4 P–KB4, 10 P–R5 P–B5, 11 B–Q2 P–KN4, 12 P–R6 B–B3, 13 N–R2 ±.

Position after 13 BxP??

A reasonable try for Black at the seventh move is an immediate liquidation of the centre, as follows: 7 . . . PxP, 8 NxP R–K1, 9 P–B3 P–B3, 10 Q–Q2 P–Q4!, 11 KPxP PxP, 12 O–O—thus far **Gligoric-Tringov,** The Hague, 1966. Now Tringov went wrong with 12 . . . N–B3?, 13 P–B5! B–Q2, 14 QR–Q1 Q–K2, 15 B–B2 QxP, 16 N–K6, etc. ±. Black's best 12th move is . . . PxP (as in **Gligoric-Fischer,** Stockholm, 1962), setting a nasty trap. For example, if 13 BxP?? then . . .

PLAY WOULD CONTINUE:

13 . . .	RxB!
14 QxR	N–KN5

and White loses the Knight on Q4.

Gligoric didn't fall for that one, of course, but nevertheless achieved no more than equality after 13 QR–Q1 P–QR3, 14 BxP P–QN4, 15 B–N3 B–N2, 16 Q–KB2 QN–Q2, 17 N–B2 Q–B2 =.

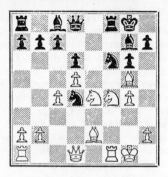

Position after 16 N–KB4?

THE OPENING MOVES WERE:

Those players who venture into extremely well analysed variations such as this one (which the Russians are fond of calling the Aronin-Taimanov System) must be familiar with every little nuance and fine point if they hope to keep a whole skin. In the diagrammed position, Black has wandered unawares into a line played in the game **Petrosian-Tal**, Bled, 1961. On the 16th move Petrosian chose 16 N(3)–KB2, and a draw was agreed after Tal's reply ... Q–K2. Lawman selects a different move for White ... This game was played in the British Correspondence Championship, Candidates, 1967.

	E. J. Lawman	M. W. Wills
1	P–Q4	N–KB3
2	P–QB4	P–KN3
3	N–QB3	B–N2
4	P–K4	P–Q3
5	N–B3	O–O
6	B–K2	P–K4
7	O–O	N–QB3
8	P–Q5	N–K2
9	N–K1	N–Q2
10	N–Q3	P–KB4

A very well known position. White can now choose PxP (the most popular), B–Q2, P–B3, or the text move, which is quite playable, but somewhat under a cloud these days owing to some recent badly handled games by Black. An example of good play by Black is: 11 P–B4 KPxP, 12 BxP BxN, 13 PxB PxP, 14 N–N4! N–KB4, 15 P–N4? N–R5 with considerable advantage (**Wade-Penrose**, Hastings, 1962).

11	P–B4	KPxP
12	BxP	PxP
13	NxP	N–B4
14	B–N5	N–B3!
15	P–KN4	N–Q5
16	N–KB4?	

PLAY NOW CONTINUED:

16	...	Q–K2!
17	NxN ch	BxN
18	BxB	Q–K6 ch!
19	K–N2	RxB
20	Q–Q3	QxQ
21	BxQ	BxP

with a won game for Black.

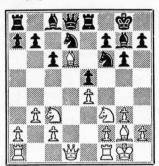

Position after 11 B–Q6?

The problem of how to keep Bobby Fischer "quiet"—i.e., in a reasonably passive position—is one which has proved insoluble to most of the world's greatest masters in recent years. At Skopje, 1967, the Russian player Kholmov tried to do it by omitting P–QB4 from the White king's fianchetto variation. This plan worked alright for the first ten moves, but then White played one "keep quiet" move too many, instead of casting around for something a little more creative.

THE OPENING MOVES WERE:

	Kholmov	Fischer
1	P–Q4	N–KB3
2	N–KB3	P–KN3
3	P–KN3	B–N2
4	B–N2	O–O
5	O–O	P–Q3
6	N–B3	QN–Q2
7	P–N3!?	

Extremely passive.

7	...	P–K4
8	PxP	PxP
9	P–K4	R–K1
10	B–QR3	

Doubtless already having in mind his faulty 11th move.

10	...	P–B3

"Telegraphing" the counterpunch ... Q–R4, so Kholmov must surely have considered it before making his next move—perhaps overlooking that his Queen will have to protect *three* important points when she gets to Q3, not just the two at QB3 and Q6.

11 B–Q6?

PLAY NOW CONTINUED:

11	...	Q–R4

As expected.

12	Q–Q3	R–K3!

Now the otherwise excellent manoeuvre 13 N–K2? will fail to ... NxP!.

13	P–QN4	

How else is the Bishop to be ex-extricated?

13	...	Q–R6
14	B–B7	QxNP

and Black has not only won a pawn, but also remains with the better position.

29

Position after 7 B–Q3?

White's idea in the Saemisch variation is to block the centre, castle Queen's
side, and drive the King's side pawns
forward in a mating attack. In the line
discussed here, Black plans to hold the
King's side with ... P–K4, followed by
... N–KR4 and ... P–KB4 if White
replies P–Q5, and then hit back with
... P–QB3 and ... PxQP. In the diagrammed position, White has delayed
7 P–Q5, and moved his KB instead.

THE OPENING MOVES WERE:

White	Black
1 P–Q4	N–KB3
2 P–QB4	P–KN3
3 N–QB3	B–N2
4 P–K4	P–Q3
5 P–B3	O–O
6 B–K3	P–K4
7 B–Q3?	

PLAY NOW CONTINUES:

7 ...	N–N5!

and White must lose at least a pawn no
matter how he wriggles. For example:
8 PxN PxP, 9 BxP (9 B–Q2 will
eventually lose a pawn to the check on
KR4) BxB, 10 P–KN3 Q–KB3!, etc.

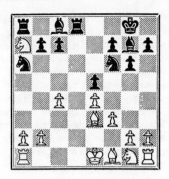

Position after 10 NxRP?

Another common error by inexperienced players at the seventh move is to exchange pawns and Queens, and then go after the vulnerable Queen's side pawns with the Knight. For example: 7 PxP PxP, 8 QxQ RxQ, 9 N–N5 N–R3, 10 NxRP? leading to the diagrammed position.

PLAY NOW CONTINUES:

10 ...   N–QN5!

regaining the pawn with considerable positional advantage.

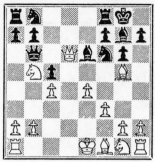

Position after 11 QxP?

THE OPENING MOVES WERE:

White can prevent the freeing manoeuvre 6 ... P–K4 by playing his QB to N5 instead of K3 on the fifth move, but in so doing he allows the powerful 6 ... P–B4. If White then replies 7 P–Q5, Black can adopt Benoni strategy by combining ... P–K3 with a Queen's side attack. In this type of variation, Black often leaves his QP unprotected for a while. The top diagram shows what can happen if White takes it.

C. Schroeder M. Wills
(Semi-finals of the Fifth ICCF Championship)

1	P–Q4	N–KB3
2	P–QB4	P–KN3
3	N–QB3	B–N2
4	P–K4	P–Q3
5	P–B3	O–O
6	B–N5	P–B4!
7	P–Q5	
7	...	P–K3
8	Q–Q2	

6 ... P–K4? loses material after 7 PxP PxP, 8 QxQ RxQ, 9 N–Q5!, etc. 7 PxP is answered by... Q–R4!

Shamkovich-Gligoric, Sarajevo, 1963, continued 8 KN–K2 P–KR3, 9 B–B4 PxP, 10 KPxP N–R4, with a good game for Black.

At this point we part company with Schroeder-Wills, which was won by Black on the 29th move (White now played 9 B–Q3!), and join **Tolush-Boleslavsky,** 20th USSR Championship.

8	...	Q–R4
9	N–N5!?	Q–N3
10	PxP	
10	...	BxP
11	QxP?	

Tolush played the questionable 10 P–QR4!?, as shown in the lower diagram.

PLAY NOW CONTINUES:

11	..	N–B3!

and 12 ... QR–Q1 is going to make life very difficult for White.

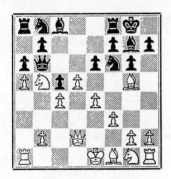

Position after 11 P–R5?

PLAY NOW CONTINUED:

Tolush-Boleslavsky actually continued 10 P–QR4!? P–QR3, 11 P–R5? (see diagram). Doubtless Tolush thought Black would have to put his Queen back on Q1, whereupon the QP could have been picked up under more favourable circumstances than mentioned above. However, White now received a nasty shock . . .

	Black	**White**
11	**. . .**	**PxN!**
12	**PxQ**	**RxR ch**
13	**K–B2**	**PxBP**

and White's King's Rook and Knight are paralysed, leaving Black with overwhelming superiority in respect to "troops immediately available for battle".

Position after 11 B–K3??

Although White's initial set-up in the Saemisch is rigid and stereotyped, it is still important that his moves be played in the order appropriate to Black's countermeasures. For example, if Black plays 4 . . . O–O instead of the usual 4 . . . P–Q3, the careless 5 P–KB3? permits the sharp sacrificial riposte . . . P–QB4! In the top diagram, White has "won" a pawn, but now fails to find the right answer to Black's multiple tactical threats.

THE OPENING MOVES WERE:

	White	Black
1	P–Q4	N–KB3
2	P–QB4	P–KN3
3	N–QB3	B–N2
4	P–K4	O–O
5	P–KB3?	

5 B–K3 is the only good move here, if White wants to play the Saemisch line.

In the game **Letelier-Fischer**, Leipzig, 1960, White tried a violent pawn rush instead, but soon found his premature attack repulsed: 5 P–K5 N–K1, 6 P–B4 P–Q3, 7 B–K3 P–QB4, 8 QPxP N–QB3, 9 BPxP PxP, 10 N–K4 B–B4, 11 N–N3 B–K3, 12 N–B3 Q–B2, 13 Q–N1 PxP, 14 P–B5 P–K5! with virtually a won game for Black.

5	. . .	P–QB4!
6	PxP	P–QN3!
7	B–K3	PxP
8	BxP	N–B3
9	Q–Q2	R–N1
10	B–Q3?	

Not realising the danger, White leaves his QR in the line of fire.

10	. . .	Q–R4
11	B–K3??	

11 B–QR3 was the only chance now, although Black would soon win the QBP because of White's QNP having to stay on the second rank to protect the Bishop.

PLAY NOW CONTINUES:

11	. . .	RxP!!

12 QxR NxKP!, 13 KN–K2 NxN, 14 B–Q2 N–QN5! and White cannot avoid ruinous loss of material.

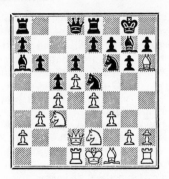

Position after 12 B–KR6?

This next example isn't really a trap, and White's disadvantage after the error is not all that great. But Black's reply to the thematic 12 B–KR6? brings about such a quaint position that I just cannot resist including it. The antagonists were **Phillips** (White) and **Penrose**, and the scene of the crime Oxford, 1967: 1 P–Q4 N–KB3, 2 P–QB4 P–KN3, 3 N–QB3 B–N2, 4 P–K4 P–Q3, 5 P–KB3 O–O, 6 KN–K2 P–B4, 7 B–K3 P–N3, 8 Q–Q2 B–QR3, 9 P–QN3 R–K1, 10 P–Q5 QN–Q2, 11 R–Q1 N–K4, 12 B–KR6?

PLAY NOW CONTINUED:

White	Black
12 ...	N–Q6 ch!

and it's mate (!) unless White takes the Knight off, so he must leave his precious QB to its fate.

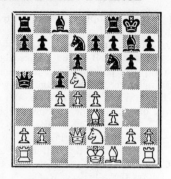

Position after 9 N-Q5?

It is a common theme, where Black plays a King's side fianchetto, for the Queen to arrive on QR4 and stay there unprotected for a while, very often vis-a-vis with the White Queen on Q2, but with a White Knight between them on QB3. The opportunity then often arises for White to play a "desperado" N-Q5, hoping to be able to check with the Knight (capturing say the Black KP at the same time) before recapturing the Queen in the event of . . . QxQ. But the plan can sometimes boomerang . . .

THE OPENING MOVES WERE:

Nilsen	Larsen
(Copenhagen, 1965)	
1 P–Q4	N–KB3
2 P–QB4	P–KN3
3 N–QB3	B–N2
4 P–K4	P–Q3
5 P–B3	O–O
6 B–K3	QN–Q2

A parting of the ways for Black. With this move he announces his intention of trying for Queen's side play, rather than central counteraction with . . . P–K4.

7 Q–Q2	P–B4
8 KN–K2	Q–R4
9 N–Q5?	

A very tempting move, since Black seems obliged to either beat a humble retreat to Q1, or assist White's Rook development by . . . QxQ ch, 10 KxQ!

PLAY NOW CONTINUED:

9 . . .	NxN!!
10 QxQ	

If 10 BPxN then Black keeps the Queens on with the awkward (for White) . . . Q–N3, since 11 PxP NxP, 12 P–QN4 fails to 12 . . . QxP!, etc.

10 . . .	NxB
11 Q–Q2	PxP

and Black's fine position plus two minor pieces and a pawn are worth more than the Queen.

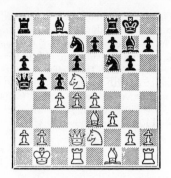

Position after 11 N–Q5?

The game **Bobotsov-Tal,** Varna, 1958, featured the same motif at a slightly later stage. This time Black chose 8 . . . P–QR3 instead of . . . Q–R4, and White continued 9 O–O–O Q–R4, 10 K–N1 P–QN4, 11 N–Q5?

PLAY NOW CONTINUED:

	White	Black
11	. . .	NxN!!
12	QxQ	NxB
13	R–B1	NxBP

and once again the Queen cannot cope with the two powerful minor pieces.

Position after 7 ... P–QB4?

One idea for Black that has gained in popularity over the last decade is to go for immediate expansion on the Queen's side, leaving the centre to White for the time being. But the defence must be conducted with great accuracy. Let us examine two points to watch for, the first involving loss of material, and the second loss of the game itself.

THE OPENING MOVES WERE:

> **Bronstein** **Lutikov**
> (USSR Championship, 1959)
> 1 P–Q4   N–KB3
> 2 P–QB4   P–KN3
> 3 N–QB3   B–N2
> 4 P–K4   P–Q3
> 5 P–B3   O–O
> 6 B–K3   P–QN3

The alternative 6 ... P–QB3 is discussed in the lower half of the page.

> 7 B–Q3   P–QB4?

This innocuous-looking move has the merit of making Lutikov's next unsound!

PLAY NOW CONTINUED:

> 8 P–K5!   N–K1
> 9 B–K4

and Black loses the exchange.

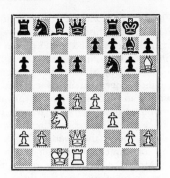

Position after 9 . . . PxP?

PLAY NOW CONTINUES:

Another risky scheme for Black is to push forward the pawn phalanx QR3–QN4–QB3 in order to discourage Queen's side castling and a direct King's side attack by White. Here again the slightest loss of tempo can prove fatal for the defence, as evidenced by the diagrammed position, where Black has taken time out to capture the QBP, doubtless thinking that after the anticipated BxP he will be able to liquidate the centre by . . . P–Q4. The opening varies from **Bronstein-Lutikov** at the sixth turn: 6 . . . P–QB3, 7 Q–Q2 P–QR3, 8 O–O–O P–QN4, 9 B–R6! PxP?

	White	Black
10	P–KR4!	P–Q4
11	P–R5	

and Black is as good as lost already.

Two possibilities are: (*a*) 11 . . . BxB, 12 QxB P–KN4!?, 13 N–R3! BxN, 14 PxB! ±; and (*b*) 11 . . . N–K1 (. . . NxRP?? is of course refuted by 12 RxN! PxR, 13 Q–N5), 12 BxB NxB, 13 RPxP BPxP, 14 Q–R6 ±.

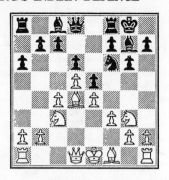

Position after 10 BxN?

When Black adopts the Panno idea against the Saemisch, and places his QN on B3 so as to have the option of ... P–K4 and ... N–Q5, or ... R–QN1 and ... P–QR3, then White's seventh and eighth moves usually have the casting vote as to which line it is to be. In the diagrammed position White has elected to attack the King's side directly with his eighth move, thus leading Black to plump for immediate counter-action in the centre—but White has made the fatal error of taking the Knight off as soon as it arrived on Q5.

THE OPENING MOVES WERE:

	Foster	Thimann
	(BCCC Candidates 1965/66)	
1	P–Q4	N–KB3
2	P–QB4	P–KN3
3	N–QB3	B–N2
4	P–K4	P–Q3
5	P–B3	O–O
6	B–K3	N–B3
7	KN–K2	P–QR3
8	N–N3	P–K4
9	P–Q5	N–Q5

(Let us now pause to consider the game **Milev-Tal**, Varna, 1962, as an example of how to deal properly with the intruder. Milev had chosen 8 N–B1 instead, and Tal replied: 8 ... P–K4, 9 P–Q5 N–Q5, 10 N–N3! (forcing Black to shift the Knight himself) NxN, 11 PxN N–R4, 12 P–QN4 P–KB4, 13 P–B5 B–B3, 14 Q–Q2 B–R5 ch, 15 K–Q1 PxKP, 16 PxKP B–Q2, with equality.)

PLAY NOW CONTINUED:

10 BxN?	PxB
11 N(3)–K2	

Obviously not 11 QxP? because of NxKP! etc.

| 11 ... | P–B4! |

Leaving White with no option but to accept the sacrifice, since otherwise the thorn at Q4 will slowly poison his whole position.

But Foster's King now becomes exposed: 12 PxP ep PxP, 13 NxP (if 13 QxP then B–K3! leaves Black miles ahead in development) Q–R4 ch, and White is as good as lost, since 14 Q–Q2 QxQ ch, 15 KxQ NxP ch, 16 NxN BxN is a winning ending for Black, and 14 K–B2 is also most unpalatable after 14 ... Q–B4! So 14 K–K2 was forced at this stage, and White soon succumbed to a mating attack.

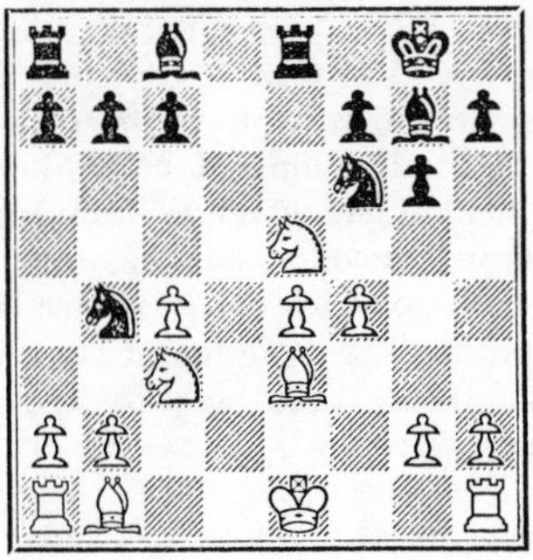

The Queen's side counterattack 6 . . .
P–QB4 has been very heavily analysed
of late, so King's Indian addicts will no
doubt be interested to examine the
latest thoughts on the sharp alternative
6 . . . P–K4. White's best play is not to
go pawn-grabbing, but instead to capture with his KBP and then lock the
centre with 8 P–Q5. However, the pawn-
grabbing lines are very tricky, and Black
has to know them well.

Position after 12 B–N1?

THE OPENING MOVES WERE:

	White	Black
1	P–Q4	N–KB3
2	P–QB4	P–KN3
3	N–QB3	B–N2
4	P–K4	P–Q3
5	P–B4	O–O
6	N–B3	P–K4?!

White's optimum strategy here is 7 BPxP PxP, 8 P–Q5! (8 NxP? is very poor—
i.e., 8 . . . P–B4!, 9 P–Q5 NxP ∓) P–B4!, 9 B–KN5! (otherwise 9 . . . N–K1 and
. . . N–Q3 is very strong for Black) P–KR3, 10 B–R4 Q–N3! Now 11 Q–Q2 N–R4,
12 B–B2! B–Q2! gives equality.

	White	Black
7	QPxP	PxP
8	QxQ	RxQ
9	NxP	R–K1!

Three reasonable lines for White are:

10 B–K3 QN–Q2, 11 NxN BxN, 12 P–K5 N–KN5, 13 B–Q4 P–KB3 =.

10 B–K2 KN–Q2, 11 NxN NxN, 12 P–K5 P–KB3, 13 PxP NxP ∓.

10 B–Q2 N–QR3, 11 B–K3! (this line is better for White than the one discussed
below, because now 11 . . . N–QN5 would not threaten a Bishop on Q3) N–KN5,
12 NxN BxN ch, 13 PxB BxN, 14 P–K5 P–KB3, with at least equality.

White's fourth alternative is . . .

	White	Black
10	B–Q3	N–QR3
11	B–K3	N–QN5
12	B–QN1?	

12 O–O–O is relatively best here.

PLAY NOW CONTINUES:

12 . . . N–KN5, 13 NxN QBxN, 14 P–QR3 QR–Q1!, and White cannot take the
Knight—and 15 . . . N–Q6 comes next, with a big plus for Black.

When White permits the freeing manoeuvre ... QBPxP in the Four Pawns variation, the game takes on many of the characteristics of a Maroczy Bind Sicilian where White has ventured P–KB4. All the familiar Sicilian tactical points can be found lurking hidden in the position. In the diagrammed position, we find Black plucking the forbidden fruit on QN7.

Position after 14 ... QxP??

THE OPENING MOVES WERE:

	Trifunovic	**Vukcevic**
	(Sarajevo, 1958)	
1	P–Q4	N–KB3
2	P–QB4	P–KN3
3	N–QB3	B–N2
4	P–K4	P–Q3
5	P–B4	O–O

(5 ... P–B4 is somewhat inferior here, a typical example being **Penrose–Gligoric,** Hastings, 1961/62: 5 ... P–B4, 6 P–Q5 O–O, 7 B–Q3 P–K3, 8 KN–K2 PxP, 9 KPxP ±. White has been able to play his KN to K2 rather than KB3, and thus stands better than he does in the usual 5 ... O–O, 6 N–B3 P–B4, 7 P–Q5 line.)

6	N–B3	P–B4
7	B–K2	PxP
8	NxP	N–B3
9	B–K3	Q–N3?
10	N–B2!	

Inviting Black to commit suicide with ... QxP??, 11 N–R4!, etc. White resists the temptation—for the time being!

10	...	Q–R4
11	O–O	N–Q2
12	N–Q4	Q–N3
13	P–K5!?	PxP
14	N–B5	QxP??

PLAY NOW CONTINUED:

15	N–QR4	Q–R6
16	B–B1	Q–N5
17	B–Q2	Q–R6
18	R–B3	

and the Poison Pawn has claimed yet another victim.

Position after 10 . . . BxB??

PLAY NOW CONTINUED:

The move 9 . . . N–KN5 is quite a reasonable proposition for Black, if followed up correctly by 10 BxN BxN!, 11 BxKB BxB, 12 QxB NxB =. But 10 . . . BxB is a horrible blunder, actually perpetrated in master play by **Mestrovic** against **Bertok** during the 1963 Yugoslav Championship.

11 NxN!	BxQ
12 NxQ	

and Black is suddenly a piece down!

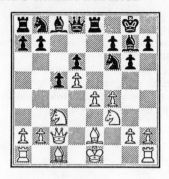

Position after 10 Q–B2?

THE OPENING MOVES WERE:

Sprocha	Fabian
(Correspondence game, 1961)	
1 P–Q4	N–KB3
2 P–QB4	P–KN3
3 N–QB3	B–N2
4 P–K4	P–Q3
5 P–B4	O–O
6 N–B3	P–B4
7 P–Q5	P–K3
8 B–K2	PxP
9 BPxP	
9 ...	R–K1

10 Q–B2?

PLAY NOW CONTINUED:

10 ...	NxKP!
11 NxN	B–B4
12 B–Q3	Q–K2
13 N–Q2	BxN
14 BxB	P–B4

The wild 9 BPxP line in this variation can also be reached via the Modern Benoni, as follows: 1 P–Q4 N–KB3, 2 P–QB4 P–B4, 3 P–Q5 P–K3, 4 N–QB3 PxP, 5 PxP P–Q3, 6 P–K4 P–KN3, 7 P–B4 B–N2, 8 N–B3 O–O, 9 B–K2 (although in practice White usually takes the opportunity of playing the ultra-sharp 8 B–N5 ch or 8 P–K5 instead). The resulting positions absolutely teem with tactical chances for both sides, so it will be fair if we examine one trap for White, and one for Black.

More easy to analyse thoroughly is 6 ... P–K4?!, as discussed on page 41.

If White's wants a positional game, he can play 9 KPxP instead.

Now White can either try to keep things on an even keel with 10 N–Q2 (although 10 ... P–B5!?, as in **Pomar-Fischer,** Havana Olympiad, 1966, needs careful handling), or try to blast a way straight through the centre with 10 P–K5!? (facing page). The move played here allows a Milan-Wills type combination.

with a fine game for Black.

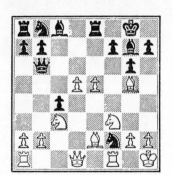

Position after 14 ... N–B7 ch?

PLAY NOW CONTINUES:

15 RxN	QxR
16 N–K4!	Q–N3
17 N–Q6	

One of the most interesting early games with 10 P–K5!? was **Mileika-Tal,** Riga, 1959, which continued: 10 ... PxP, 11 PxP N–N5, 12 P–K6 PxP, 13 O–O PxP!, 14 NxP B–K3, 15 B–QB4 N–K4!?, 16 B–KN5 NxN ch, 17 QxN QxB, 18 QR–K1 R–KB1, 19 RxB? B–Q5 ch ∓ (although, as is often the case with Tal, it was realised *after* the game that 19 QxR ch BxQ, 20 RxB would have been much better). White's best 12th move of all is probably B–KN5, which sets a little trap: 12 ... Q–N3, 13 O–O! P–B5 dis ch, 14 K–R1 N–B7 ch?

regaining the exchange with a crushing attack.

Position after 13 ... BxR?

A common theme in the 4 PxP variation is the possibility of an exchange sacrifice by White, the QR being traded for the Black KB after P–Q5 at some opportune moment. Very often it is best for Black to refuse the offer altogether. In the diagrammed position, we examine one of the earliest known instances of the sacrifice.

THE OPENING MOVES WERE:

	Sokolsky	Tolush
	(Omsk, 1944)	
1	P–Q4	N–KB3
2	P–QB4	P–KN3
3	N–QB3	P–Q4
4	PxP	NxP
5	P–K4	NxN
6	PxN	B–N2
7	B–QB4	P–QB4
8	N–K2	PxP
9	PxP	N–QB3
10	B–K3	O–O
11	O–O	N–R4
12	B–Q3	B–K3?
13	P–Q5!	BxR??

There is no absolute obligation to take the Rook (other than the moral one!), as was demonstrated in the game **Fuderer-Mesicek**, Maribor, 1950, which continued B–KN5, 14 R–QB1 P–QN3, 15 P–KR3 B–B1, 16 N–Q4 P–K3, 17 N–B6 NxN, 18 PxN Q–B2 with only slight advantage to White.

PLAY NOW CONTINUED:

14	QxB	P–KB3
15	B–R6	R–K1
16	N–KB4	B–Q2
17	P–K5	

and White won very quickly.

The alternative 16 ... B–B2 is somewhat stronger, although even then White retains a big plus after 17 B–QN5 Q–Q3, 18 BxR RxB, 19 Q–B3 P–N3, 20 R–QB1 (**Einevoldsen-Flores**, Dubrovnik, 1950).

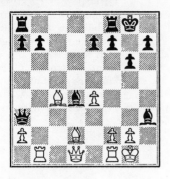

Position after 15 ... BxKRP?

When White takes his opportunity to build up a big centre against the Grunfeld, there are certain basic precepts of opening play which need modification if the mighty structure is to be properly sustained. For example, where one might think that "Knights belong on B3" is a very good maxim to follow always, it certainly doesn't apply to the White KN in this variation of the Grunfeld. Nevertheless, Black must be careful not to overdo things.

THE OPENING MOVES WERE:

	White	Black
1	P–Q4	N–KB3
2	P–QB4	P–KN3
3	N–QB3	P–Q4
4	PxP	NxP
5	P–K4	NxN
6	PxN	P–QB4
7	B–QB4	B–N2
8	N–B3!?	
8	...	N–B3

The correct move here is 8 N–K2.

It is not the actual pin that does the damage in this variation (and indeed it loses outright if played at once—e.g., 8 ... B–KN5??, 9 BxP ch!, etc.) but the *threat* of it.

9	B–K3	O–O
10	P–KR3	PxP
11	PxP	Q–R4 ch
12	B–Q2?	

The bizarre 12 K–K2 seems best here.

12	...	Q–R6
13	O–O	

There is nothing else.

13	...	NxP
14	NxN	BxN
15	R–N1	BxKRP?

But this is *not* the right move, although many quite recent books give it an exclamation mark. Correct is 15 ... P–QR4, cutting out B–QN4 and retaining the pawn without any real disadvantage.

PLAY NOW CONTINUES:

16 R–N3! (and not 16 PxB because of ... Q–N6 ch, 17 K–R1 QxP ch, 18 K–N1 B–K4!, etc.), Q–B4, 17 B–Q5! and Black hasn't time to prevent the deadly B–QN4.

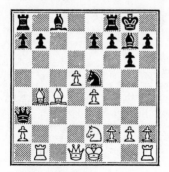

Position after 14 B–N4??

PLAY NOW CONTINUES:

One very similar line where White *does* come to grief is: 8 N–K2 N–B3, 9 B–K3 PxP, 10 PxP Q–R4 ch, 11 B–Q2 Q–R6, 12 R–QN1 O–O, 13 P–Q5? (13 O–O is more circumspect) N–K4, 14 B–N4??

14 ...   **Q–KB6!!**

and White gets mated if he takes the Queen, so he must castle instead and let Black take the KP for nothing.

49

Position after 8 QxNP?

The very early Q–N3 forces an immediate decision on Black—should he choose the rather passive . . . P–QB3, or surrender the centre with . . . PxP. In the latter variation, Black can hit the Queen straight away with 5 . . . B–K3 if he is familiar with the complicated lines which follow upon 6 Q–N5 ch. The general consensus of opinion among the pundits is that the 4 Q–N3 system as a whole tends to favour Black. In the top diagrammed position, we find the White Queen engaged in the well-known (and suspect) pastime of pawn-snatching.

THE OPENING MOVES WERE:

White	Black
1 P–Q4	N–KB3
2 P–QB4	P–KN3
3 N–QB3	P–Q4
4 Q–N3	PxP
5 QxBP	B–K3
6 Q–N5 ch	

6 Q–Q3 is perfectly alright for White, although Black can equalise quite easily with the temporary pawn sacrifice 6 . . . P–QB4!

6 . . .	N–QB3
7 N–KB3	N–Q4!

Definitely the best here. If Black merely continues with his fianchetto, White can grab the pawn and then scamper back home with impunity. For example, 7 . . . B–N2?, 8 QxNP B–Q2, 9 Q–N3 R–QN1, 10 Q–Q1 (**Euwe-Landau,** 1939). Nor is 7 . . . R–QN1? to be recommended, because of the powerful reply 8 P–K4!

8 QxNP?

PLAY NOW CONTINUES:

8 . . .	N(4)–N5!
9 Q–N5	B–Q2

Threatening 9 . . . R–QN1.
and White cannot cope with the multiple threats . . . N–B7 ch, . . . NxQP, and . . . QR–QN1.

On the ninth move, White can also try 9 B–KB4 (as in **Sokor-Volck,** 1937), but this also fails after 9 . . . B–KR3!!, 10 BxP NxQP!, 11 BxQ N(Q5)–B7 ch, 12 K–Q1 RxB ch, and the game is over.

Another trap at White's eighth move is 8 N–K5 ?, which seeks to take advantage of the unprotected state of Black's King's Rook after ensuing exchanges. (In passing, it is worth noting that White's safest line here is 8 NxN BxN, 9 P–K3, etc.)

Position after 8 N–K5 ?

PLAY NOW CONTINUES:

8 ...		N(4)–N5!	
9	NxN	N–B7 ch	
10	K–Q1	PxN	
11	Q–K5		or 11 QxP ch? B–Q2!, etc.
11 ...		QxP ch	
12	QxQ	NxQ	with a safe pawn in the bag.

Position after 7 Q–R4 ch?

THE OPENING MOVES WERE:

	White	Black
1	P–Q4	N–KB3
2	P–QB4	P–KN3
3	P–KN3	B–N2
4	B–N2	P–Q4
5	PxP	NxP
6	P–K4	N–N5
7	Q–R4 ch?	

When White chooses not to develop his QN at move 3, it leaves him the option of playing 6 P–K4 without allowing the exchange of Knights which usually takes place. Black can then proceed on positional lines by . . . N–QN3, or tactically with . . . N–QN5. The latter variation is extremely complex and difficult for both sides. Two typical snares must serve to illustrate the many possibilities, since a complete analysis of the line is outside the scope of this book.

White hopes to win a piece by pushing his QP to threaten whichever Knight goes to QB3, and also wishes to avoid the veiled threat to his QB2 square (e.g., 7 N–K2? BxP!, 8 NxB QxN!!, 9 QxQ N–B7 ch, etc.). A better line is that mentioned on the facing page.

PLAY NOW CONTINUES:

7	. . .	N(1)–QB3
8	P–Q5	P–QN4!
9	QxNP	B–QR3
10	Q–R4	O–O

and White is in a terrible mess.

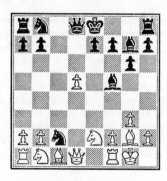

Position after 10 ... N–B7?

White's sharpest line at move 7 is P–Q5 (although the quiet 7 P–QR3 is also good), and this leads to very interesting play if Black hits the advanced pawn at once, with 7 ... P–QB3, 8 N–K2 PxP, 9 PxP B–B4. Now once again 10 Q–R4 ch? would be futile, because after ... N(1)–QB3! Black is threatening ... B–B7. White should instead castle (!), leaving QB2 without apparent protection. But Black can do nothing about the "weakness". For example ...

PLAY NOW CONTINUES:

11 P–KN4!	NxR
12 PxB	

and Black's Knight will never get out alive.

Strangely enough, the Zwischenzug* of the KNP can be a *mistake* on the very next move. For example, if Black avoids the snare and just castles, and the game continues 11 QN–QB3 N(1)–QR3, then 12 P–KN4? is answered not by 12 ... BxP?, 13 P–QR3! winning a piece, but by 12 ... B–B7!, 13 Q–Q2 N–B4 with a tremendous grip on the position.

* *A German word meaning "nasty, underhand intermediary move".*

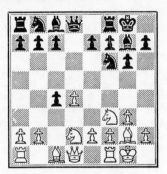

Position after 7 QN–Q2?

One of the most prolific innovators of modern times is the Russian theorist Y. Estrin. Countless variations have been subjected to close scrutiny in his study, later to appear transformed in literally hundreds of articles contributed to the numerous chess magazines of the world. These new discoveries are often of assistance in his over-the-board chess also—the diagrammed position illustrates a typical instance.

THE OPENING MOVES WERE:

	Kimelfeld	Estrin
	(Semi-finals of the USSR	
	Championship 1968)	
1	P–Q4	N–KB3
2	P–QB4	P–KN3
3	P–KN3	B–N2
4	B–N2	P–Q4
5	N–KB3	O–O
6	O–O	PxP
7	QN–Q2?	

It is hard luck on Kimelfeld that he has to be the first one to find out that this move actually merits a question mark. Previous learned tomes have recommended this move as leading to a nice even game. For example: **Pogrevenski-Greshkin,** Semi-finals of the USSR Championship 1949: 7 QN–Q2 P–QN4, 8 P–N3 P–B6, 9 N–N1 B–N2?, 10 NxP P–QR3, 11 B–QR3 QN–Q2, 12 R–QB1 R–K1, 13 Q–B2 R–QB1, etc. =. But Estrin has been doing some homework on this game!

PLAY NOW CONTINUED:

7	...	P–QN4!
8	P–N3	

The superficially attractive 8 N–K5? allows the shock reply 8 ... QxP!, 9 BxR QxN, with plenty of stuff in hand for the exchange, and a powerful grip on the centre.

8	...	P–B6
9	N–N1	P–N5!
10	P–QR3	P–QB4!
11	N–N5	N–Q4
12	QPxP	B–N2
13	R–R2	P–QR4

and Black is virtually a piece up, in view of the entombed state of White's QN.

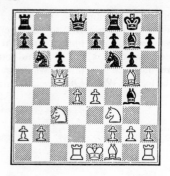

Position after 11 B–KN5?

One of Fischer's first victories in top-class chess, against D. Byrne at New York, 1956, serves as an excellent illustration of the perils awaiting White if he fails to get castled before Black begins his thematic advance on the Queen's side. In the Q–N3 variation White spends a lot of time placing his pieces in good positions at the centre of the board, but nevertheless should always be able to tuck his King away before any trouble develops, *if* he plays correctly.

THE OPENING MOVES WERE:

	D. Byrne	Fischer
1	N–KB3	N–KB3
2	P–B4	P–KN3
3	N–B3	B–N2
4	P–Q4	O–O
5	B–B4	P–Q4
6	Q–N3	PxP
7	QxBP	P–B3
8	P–K4	QN–Q2
9	R–Q1	N–N3
10	Q–B5	

Byrne takes his 14(!)-year-old opponent too lightly.—10 Q–N3 is best here.

10 . . .	B–N5
11 B–KN5?	

PLAY NOW CONTINUED:

11 . . .	N–R5!
12 Q–R3	

If White takes the Knight, then 12 . . . NxP slices his position open with great advantage to Black. For example, 13 QxKP QxQ, 14 BxQ KR–K1, etc.; or 13 Q–N4 NxB, 14 NxN BxR, 15 KxB BxP, etc.

12 . . .	NxN
13 PxN	NxP!

and White must eventually lose material.

The game continued 14 BxP Q–N3, 15 B–QB4 NxQBP!, 16 B–B5 KR–K1 ch, 17 K–B1 B–K3!! and White had to accept the Queen sacrifice, with the sequel 18 BxQ BxB ch, 19 K–N1 N–K7 ch, 20 K–B1 NxP dis ch, 21 K–N1 N–K7 ch, 22 K–B1 N–B6 dis ch, 23 K–N1 PxB, 24 Q–N4 R–R5, 25 QxP (if 25 Q–Q6 then NxR, 26 QxN RxP leaves White with no defence to . . . R–R8) NxR, and Black's material plus clinched victory on the 40th move.

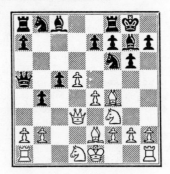

In this diagram, we examine the result of failure to castle at the twelfth move—and on the opposite page it is demonstrated that the apparently safe Q3 square can sometimes have its drawbacks for the White Queen.

Position after 12 P–Q5?

THE OPENING MOVES WERE:

	White	Black
1	P–Q4	N–KB3
2	P–QB4	P–KN3
3	N–QB3	P–Q4
4	N–KB3	B–N2
5	Q–N3	PxP
6	QxBP	O–O
7	P–K4	P–QB3
8	B–KB4	P–QN4

The alternative 8 . . . Q–R4 is discussed on the facing page.

	White	Black
9	Q–Q3	Q–R4
10	B–K2	P–N5
11	N–Q1	P–QB4!
12	P–Q5?	

12 O–O is the only good move here.

PLAY NOW CONTINUES:

	White	Black
12	. . .	B–QR3
13	Q–B2	P–N6 dis ch
14	Q–B3	Q–N3!

and White hasn't got time to exchange Bishops because of the veiled threat to his Queen from the fianchettoed Bishop. So the Queen must move again, and both . . . QxNP and . . . Q–K3 leave Black with a considerable advantage in position.

Position after 10 Q-Q3?

If Black moves his Queen out *before* pushing the QNP, the square Q3 becomes a dangerous spot for the White Queen. For example, 8 ... Q-R4, 9 B-Q2?! (not too bad on its own, but disastrous in combination with White's next) P-QN4, 10 Q-Q3? (White's game is quite tenable after Q-B5 or Q-N3, although the initiative has passed to Black).

PLAY NOW CONTINUES:

10 ...	P-N5
11 N-Q1	P-QB4
12 P-Q5	P-K3!
13 P-Q6	

trying at all costs, with this and the previous move, to keep the position closed.

| 13 ... | B-N2! |

and Black is bound to win material soon.

Position after 11 ... P–N5??

The Moscow 1963 tournament featured an attempt, by Vladimirov, to improve on White's play in a well-known variation where Black pins the QN with 9 ... Q–R4. The usual un-pinning procedures are 10 B–Q2 and 10 O–O, but White tried 10 P–K5 instead. As it happens, it induced a terrible blunder by his opponent Liberson on the 11th move—but Vladimirov overlooked the winning reply (which would have won a whole piece) ... certainly a very rare occurrence in master play.

THE OPENING MOVES WERE:

	Vladimirov	Liberson
1	P–Q4	N–KB3
2	P–QB4	P–KN3
3	N–QB3	P–Q4
4	N–B3	B–N2
5	Q–N3	PxP
6	QxBP	O–O
7	P–K4	P–B3

Probably the most popular variation here is Smyslov's ... B–N5, to be followed by ... KN–Q2, but the text move is perfectly sound.

8	B–K2	P–QN4
9	Q–N3	Q–R4
10	P–K5!?	

The alternative O–O is discussed on the facing page.

10	...	B–K3
11	Q–B2	P–N5??

What actually happened now was 12 Q–R4?, missing the win.

PLAY SHOULD HAVE CONTINUED:

12	PxN	PxN
13	P–QN4!	

and Black must lose a piece.

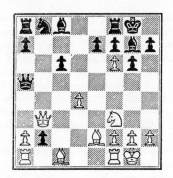

Position after 12 ... PxP?

PLAY NOW CONTINUES:

If White chooses 10 O–O instead, then 11 P–K5 is an effective reply to Black's 10 ... P–N5. Play normally proceeds 11 ... PxN, 12 PxN BxP, 13 PxP B–R3!, 14 BxB NxB, 15 R–N1 P–B4 with equality (**Najdorf-Flohr,** Stockholm, 1948). One pitfall which Black must avoid is 12 ... PxP?, which looks as if it wins a pawn in view of the threat of ... PxR = Q.

13 PxB!	PxR = Q
14 PxR = Q ch	KxQ
15 B–R6 ch	

and 16 RxQ, winning a piece.

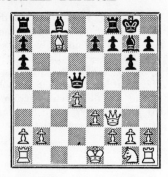

Position after 10 Q–B3?

When these top flight correspondence players really get to work on an opening variation, the whole thing eventually becomes just a clinging morass of traps and countertraps. The postal predators take particular pleasure in turning what was previously regarded as a favourable line, for one side, into virtually a forced loss. The diagrammed position arose during a game in a recent German Correspondence Championship, with White no doubt looking forward to a promising middlegame as laid down by previous theory.

THE OPENING MOVES WERE:

	de Carbonel	Koch
1	P–Q4	N–KB3
2	P–QB4	P–KN3
3	N–QB3	P–Q4
4	B–B4	

An ancient line recommended by Grunfeld himself as best for White.

	de Carbonel	Koch
4	...	B–N2
5	P–K3	O–O

Offering the pawn at QB2 in the interests of speedy development.

	de Carbonel	Koch
6	PxP	NxP
7	NxN	QxN
8	BxP	N–R3
9	BxN	

The poor alternative 9 B–N3? is discussed on the facing page.

	de Carbonel	Koch
9	...	PxB
10	Q–B3?	

Black "normally" picks off the KNP first, before recapturing on QR3 (i.e., 9 ... QxKNP, 10 Q–B3 QxQ, 11 NxQ PxB), so de Carbonel may have thought he was saving himself a pawn with this manoeuvre.

PLAY NOW CONTINUED:

    10 ...   Q–QN4!   and suddenly White is in difficulties.

(For example, the Rook is obviously taboo, because of 11 QxR? QxP, 12 R–Q1 B–N5!, 13 QxP Q–B6 ch, etc.—and 11 Q–K2? loses to 11 ... Q–N2!, 12 ... QxNP and 13 ... B–N2. White actually played 11 N–K2, but Black pressed home the attack with ... Q–N5 ch, 12 N–B3 B–N2, 13 Q–K2 BxNP, 14 R–KN1 B–B6!, 15 Q–Q2 QR–B1, 16 R–N3 B–R4, 17 B–B4 KR–Q1 ∓.

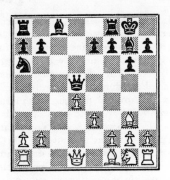

Position after 9 B–KN3?

Would-be students of the variation should note that White dare not leave Black's QN on the board at the ninth move, with 9 B–KN3?

PLAY NOW CONTINUES:

9 . . .   **B–B4!**

followed by either 10 . . . N–N5 or . . . QR–B1–B7 depending on White's reply—in both cases with considerable advantage.

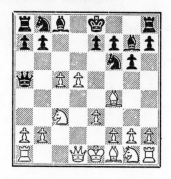

Position after 7 PxP?

THE OPENING MOVES WERE:

In this line Black gets the chance to offer the sacrifice of two pawns, but White can never take them both and hang on to the material with any degree of safety. The diagrammed position came about during the Darga-Pachman game, at Amsterdam, 1964. With his last move (7 PxP?) White gives up all hope of a win, since Black can immediately force a repetition of moves. (Whether the move merited a question mark in this particular game is a moot point, since the position is pretty well known from previous master games, and White may have played it as a "peace overture"!)

	Darga	Pachman
1	P–Q4	N–KB3
2	P–QB4	P–KN3
3	N–QB3	P–Q4
4	B–B4	B–N2
5	P–K3	P–QB4!?

Somewhat questionable (that is, unless the players have agreed to a pre-arranged draw already!), since White can retain the initiative at the seventh move with 7 Q–N3 O–O, 8 Q–N5! QxQ, 9 PxQ B–B4, 10 R–Q1 QN–Q2, 11 P–B6 PxP, 12 PxP N–N3, 13 B–R6, as in **Kluger-Pachman,** Bucharest, 1954.

6	PxBP	Q–R4
7	PxP?	

PLAY NOW CONTINUES:

7	...	NxP!
8	QxN	BxN ch

and White cannot safely avoid the draw after 9 PxB QxP ch, 10 K–K2 QxR, 11 B–K5 Q–B8!, 12 BxR B–K3, 13 QxP Q–B7 ch with perpetual check.

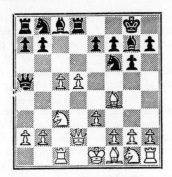

A similar position can also arise if White mishandles the 5 . . . O–O, 6 R–QB1 P–QB4, 7 PxBP Q–R4, 8 PxP R–Q1, line in the same variation. In the lower diagram White has just played the "obvious" 9 Q–Q2? (9 B–B4 is best, with the possible sequel 9 . . . B–K3!, 10 P–QN4! QxNP, 11 Q–N3 QxQ, 12 BxQ =). The game in question is **Tolush-Botvinnik,** USSR Championship, 1939.

Position after 9 Q–Q2?

PLAY NOW CONTINUED:

9 . . .	NxP
10 B–B7	QxB
11 NxN	RxN!!

and White's chronic lack of development soon proved fatal, as follows:

12 QxR B–K3, 13 Q–Q2 N–B3, 14 R–Q1 R–Q1, 15 Q–B1 Q–R4 ch, 16 R–Q2 R–Q4!, 17 N–K2 RxP, 18 N–B3 BxN, 19 PxB RxP, 20 Q–N2 R–R6, 21 Q–N5 Q–B6, 22 Q–N2 Q–B4, 23 Q–N1 BxP!, 24 RxB Q–R4 ch and wins.

Position after 6 NxP??

In the minds of some people, the words "Grunfeld Defence" conjure up a vision of some super-strategist, like Smyslov, probing gently away at a massive White centre throughout the whole of an extremely dull and lengthy middlegame, succeeding at length in provoking some minute positional weakness or other to nurture during the course of an extremely dull and lengthy ending. But sudden-death variations do exist, particularly where White departs from modern practice.

THE OPENING MOVES WERE:

	White	Black
1	P–Q4	N–KB3
2	P–QB4	P–KN3
3	N–QB3	P–Q4
4	N–B3	B–N2
5	B–KN5!?	

Inviting Black to come to grips at once, but in doing so giving up White's rightful opening initiative.

5 ...	N–K5
6 NxP??	

Snatching up the gauntlet.

See facing page for a discussion of the correct move 6 PxP.

PLAY NOW CONTINUES:

6 ...	NxB
7 NxN	P–K3!

and White is going to lose a piece already! This elementary trap has never caught a master yet, according to all known theory—but there's always a first time.

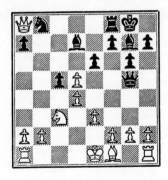

Position after 12 QxR?

Now, after that little sweetener, let's move on to the main course, consisting of one of the most complex opening variations known to theory. Suppose White plays sensibly 6 PxP, and Black replies ... NxB, 7 NxN P–K3. Things don't *have* to start happening now, but they will if White tries to upset Black with 8 Q–R4 ch!?, reasoning that ... B–Q2 can be answered by 9 Q–N3. The point is that Black *can* play ... B–Q2 (although in fact ... P–B3! is even stronger), and follow it up with the sacrifice of the QR—if White is mad enough to take it. One typical line will have to suffice in a book of this nature.

Play proceeds 9 Q–N3 QxN, 10 QxP O–O, 11 P–K3! (11 QxR at once is obviously really terrible for White after 11 ... N–B3, threatening 12 ... NxP) P–QB4! This is a critical position, where White might conceivably be able to hold on by not taking the Rook. If he does capture it ...

PLAY NOW CONTINUES:

12 ...	QBPxP!

so as to answer 13 KPxP with ... N–B3!, etc.

13 N–Q1	QPxP
14 NxP	BxP
15 R–QN1	Q–K4!

and there is no adequate defence to the combined threats of ... N–B3, ... B–B6 ch, ... PxP, and ... Q–B6 ch. Work it out for yourself—the numerous variations are quite simple.

Black's idea in this line is to provoke P–K4 by White, and then bring pressure to bear on the Queen's Pawn by shifting his KN round to QN3 via Q2, either before or after ... B–KN5. The play involved can be very tricky. This page examines one typical trap for Black.

Position after 9 ... N–QR4?

THE OPENING MOVES WERE:

White	Black
1 P–Q4	N–KB3
2 P–QB4	P–KN3
3 N–QB3	P–Q4
4 N–KB3	B–N2
5 Q–N3	PxP
6 QxBP	O–O
7 P–K4	B–KN5
8 B–K3!	
8 ...	N–QB3
9 P–Q5!	N–QR4?

Now Black's best modus operandi is the manoeuvre ... KN–Q2–N3.

PLAY NOW CONTINUES:

10 Q–R4	P–QB3
11 R–Q1!!	

and White wins material, because if the Black Queen moves off the file to avoid the veiled threat (11 ... Q–B2), the piece-winning manoeuvre 12 P–QN4 can no longer be parried by ... NxKP, NxN BxR.

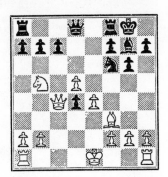

Position after 13 N–N5?

PLAY NOW CONTINUES:

If White selects the move 8 B–K2 instead, then 8 ... N–QB3, 9 B–K3 BxN! contains a little dash of poison. For example, if White recaptures the "natural" way, with 10 BxB?, Black can continue with the forceful 10 ... P–K4!, 11 P–Q5 N–Q5! Now it is not hard to see that 12 BxN PxB, 13 QxQP? fails to 13 ... NxKP! etc. Much harder to spot, though, is exactly what is wrong with 13 N–N5?

13 ...	R–K1!
14 QxBP	NxKP
15 QxQ	QRxQ
16 N–B7	R–K2

and White has nothing better than 17 BxN RxN ch, 18 K moves, leaving Black in complete control of the centre.

67

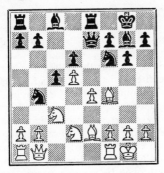

Position after 13 N-Q2?

When the inevitable pressure comes to bear upon White's KP, he must conduct its defence with the utmost accuracy if he wishes to preserve his opening initiative. The diagrammed position arose during the game Donner-Robatsch, Beverwijk, 1963, after White had carelessly answered ... Q-K2 with the obvious 13 N-Q2? Now White's centre crumbled away under the impact of several sharp combinative blows.

THE OPENING MOVES WERE:

	Donner	Robatsch
1	P-Q4	N-KB3
2	P-QB4	P-QB4
3	P-Q5	P-K3
4	N-QB3	PxP
5	PxP	P-Q3
6	P-K4	P-KN3
7	N-KB3	B-N2
8	B-K2	O-O
9	O-O	R-K1
10	Q-B2	N-QR3
11	B-KB4	N-QN5
12	Q-N1	Q-K2

Also playable is the wild 12 ... NxKP!?, as in **Averbach-Tal,** Riga, 1958, which continued: 13 NxN B-KB4, 14 KN-Q2 NxP, 15 BxP? (15 B-KN3! leaves Black to justify his sacrifice—a difficult task) N-KB3!, and Black regained his piece with a won game.

13 N-Q2?

13 R-K1 is correct here, so as to be able to answer ... NxKP? with 14 B-QN5! etc.

PLAY NOW CONTINUED:

13 ...		KNxQP!!	A fine stroke.
14	PxN	B-KB4	
15	Q-Q1		There is nowhere else for her majesty to go.

Now Black soon established a winning advantage: 15 ... BxN, 16 PxB NxQP, 17 B-QN5 NxB, 18 BxR RxB, 19 R-K1 N-R6 ch!, 20 PxN Q-N4 ch, 21 K-R1 RxR ch, 22 QxR BxKRP, 23 Q-K4 QxN etc.

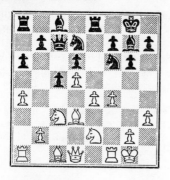

Position after 12 ... R–K1?

Without doubt, the most sensational victory by any British player in recent years was that scored by Jonathan Penrose against Tal, during the Leipzig Olympics. It was the only game lost by the entire Soviet team, Tal's first defeat since winning the world championship from Botvinnik, and the only defeat this century of a reigning world champion by a British player. The move that started Tal on the downward path to disaster was 12 ... R–K1, although the critical breakthrough by White occurred several moves later.

THE OPENING MOVES WERE:

	Penrose	Tal
1	P–Q4	N–KB3
2	P–QB4	P–K3
3	N–QB3	P–B4
4	P–Q5	PxP
5	PxP	P–Q3
6	P–K4	P–KN3
7	B–Q3	B–N2
8	KN–K2	O–O
9	O–O	P–QR3
10	P–QR4	Q–B2
11	P–R3	QN–Q2
12	P–B4	R–K1?

Tal himself said afterwards that this is where Black starts to go wrong. Better to leave the Rook on KB1 for defensive purposes and proceed immediately with Queen's side counterplay.

PLAY NOW CONTINUED:

13 N–N3

So as to bring the Queen quickly to KB3.

13	...	P–B5
14	B–B2	N–B4
15	Q–B3	KN–Q2
16	B–K3	P–QN4
17	PxP	R–N1
18	Q–B2!	

Tucking the Queen safely away so that Black will not be able to hit back effectively with ... P–K5 after capturing on K4 in reply to White's next (see facing page).

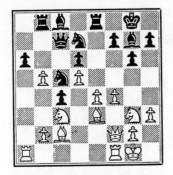

Tal captured the Queen's Knight's Pawn with 18 ... PxP, and Penrose continued 19 P–K5! PxP, 20 P–B5!!— Black was now virtually paralysed by the two pawns on the fifth rank.

Position after 18 Q–B2!

PLAY CONTINUED:

20 ...	B–N2
21 QR–Q1!	B–QR1
22 QN–K4	N–R5
23 BxN	PxB
24 PxP	BPxP
25 Q–B7 ch	

And now, with the QN ready to pene-trate the position, this move is a killer.

25 ...	K–R1
26 N–QB5	

Threatening the deadly N–K6, so Tal must give up a piece.

26 ...	Q–R2
27 QxN	QxQ
28 NxQ	RxP
29 N–N6	R–N6
30 NxQBP	

and it is all over.

The remaining moves were: 30 ... R–Q1, 31 P–Q6 R–B6, 32 QR–B1 RxR, 33 RxR B–Q4, 34 N–N6 B–N6, 35 N–K4 P–R3, 36 P–Q7 B–B1, 37 R–B8 Resigns. A great game by Penrose.

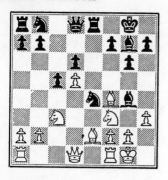

Position after 11 ... NxKP?

There was curious parallel between the Korchnoi-Lutikov and Geller-Tal games at Tiflis, 1959 (the 26th USSR Championship). Korchnoi and Geller played differently at the eighth move, but an almost exactly similar position arose just afterwards, the important feature as far as Geller was concerned being the presence of a Black pawn on QR3. This made Korchnoi's P–KR3 strong, whereas the same move in the other game would have been a blunder! Let us examine Korchnoi-Lutikov first.

THE OPENING MOVES WERE:

	Korchnoi	**Lutikov**
1	P–Q4	N–KB3
2	P–QB4	P–B4
3	P–Q5	P–K3
4	N–QB3	PxP
5	PxP	P–Q3
6	P–K4	P–KN3
7	N–B3	B–N2
8	B–K2	

Geller selected 8 B–KN5 at this point, and came back to KB4 only after Tal's 9 ... P–KR3.

8	...	O–O
9	O–O	B–N5
10	B–KB4	R–K1
11	P–KR3!	

Now Lutikov must have erroneously concluded that the combination against White's B on K2, which works well on the facing page, would also work well here.

| 11 | ... | NxKP? |

PLAY NOW CONTINUED:

| 12 | PxB | BxN |
| 13 | B–QN5! | |

This Zwischenzug, unplayable in Geller-Tal, refutes Black's idea of 13 PxB NxQBP and ... NxB ch. Lutikov struggled on, but was soon in a lost position.

13	...	BxP
14	BxR	QxB
15	R–K1!	BxR
16	QxB	P–B4
17	B–R6	

and Black had little to hope for.

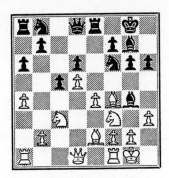

Geller-Tal varied at the eighth, as follows: 8 B–KN5 P–QR3, 9 P–QR4 P–R3, 10 B–KB4 B–N5, 11 B–K2 O–O, 12 O–O R–K1. Now Geller saw the danger in time, and avoided it by 13 Q–B2 etc. If he had followed Korchnoi's example and played 13 P–KR3?, then . . .

Position after 13 P–KR3?

PLAY WOULD HAVE CONTINUED:

13 . . .	NxKP
14 PxB	BxN
15 PxB	NxQBP
16 Q moves	NxB ch etc.

So once again we find the ubiquitous . . . NxKP involved in trappy play.

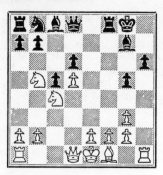

Position after 13 N–QN5??

Where White decides on straightforward piece development rather than P–K4 at the sixth turn, the character of the ensuing play is very much influenced by the square chosen for the QB on the seventh move. In the top diagram we have a position resulting from 7 B–KN5, a line introduced into grandmaster practice by Botvinnik against Tal, at Moscow, 1960.

THE OPENING MOVES WERE:

	Botvinnik	Tal
1	P–Q4	N–KB3
2	P–QB4	P–QB4
3	P–Q5	P–K3
4	N–QB3	PxP
5	PxP	P–Q3
6	N–KB3	P–KN3
7	B–KN5	B–N2

No need for Black to worry about whether he ought to play ... P–QR3 first (as he should against B–KB4), since 8 Q–R4 ch is not so strong when the Black QP remains unattacked.

8	N–Q2	P–KR3
9	B–R4	P–KN4
10	B–N3	N–KR4
11	N–QB4	

11 Q–R4 ch would have been an interesting try here—possibly Tal intended ... K–B1 in reply.

11	...	NxB
12	RPxN	O–O

Now Tal played 13 P–K3, and an even position resulted after ... Q–K2, 14 B–K2 R–Q1. A lesser mortal might well chase the Black QP with ...

13 N–QN5??

PLAY WOULD THEN CONTINUE:

13 ... P–QR3!, 14 N(5)xP P–QN4, 15 NxB PxN!, and the other venturesome cavalier is trapped on the eighth rank.

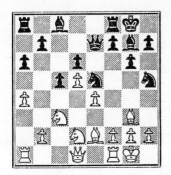

Position after 13 ... N–KR4??

In the game **Djurasevic-Bogdano-vic,** Sarajevo, 1958; White played 7 B–KB4 instead, and a tricky position arose after the continuation ... P–QR3, 8 P–K4 B–N2, 9 B–K2 O–O, 10 P–QR4 Q–K2, 11 N–Q2 QN–Q2, 12 O–O N–K4, 13 B–KN3. Bogdanovic now baited a trap with 13 ... N–KR4?, hoping that White would fall for 14 BxN PxB, 15 QxP?? B–KN5!, 16 Q–R4 B–B3, 17 Q–R6 B–N4 winning the Queen.

PLAY NOW CONTINUED:

14	BxN	PxB
15	BxN!	QxB
16	N–QB4	Q–B5
17	QxP!	B–KN5
18	Q–R4	B–B3
19	N–K2!	

and White was hoist on his own petard.

Position after 8 P–KR4?

The game between Bondarevsky and Vasyukov, in the semi-finals of the 26th Championship of the USSR, featured an interesting new attempt by White to refute Black's strategy out of hand by a direct attack on the KR file. It failed on that occasion, but might well repay further study as a means of upsetting a solid defensive player.

THE OPENING MOVES WERE:

	Bondarevsky	**Vasyukov**
1	P–Q4	N–KB3
2	P–QB4	P–QB4
3	P–Q5	P–K3
4	N–QB3	PxP
5	PxP	P–Q3
6	P–K4	P–KN3
7	B–K2	B–N2
8	P–KR4?	

PLAY NOW CONTINUED:

8	...	O–O
9	P–R5	P–QN4!
10	PxP	

10 BxP? fails to ... NxP!, 11 NxN Q–R4 ch etc.—a familiar theme in Benoni positions.

10	...	P–N5!
11	PxP ch	K–R1
12	N–N1	NxP
13	N–KB3	N–Q2
14	Q–B2	QN–B3
15	O–O	B–N2
16	N–R4	Q–Q2!

Black's pieces move smoothly into menacing positions, while White struggles to compensate for his bad position by tactical means.

17	P–KN4!?	NxQP!

with a won game. If White takes the Knight, then 18 ... N–B6 leaves the Queen with no good square to go to.

Position after 10 BxP?

The pawn exchange on White's Q5 leaves the square QB4 available for his King's Knight. In return, Black is more easily able to set a pawn roller in motion on the Queen's wing. The line discussed here shows White trying to hold back Black's latent flank expansion by early moves of the Queen and Queen's Bishop.

THE OPENING MOVES WERE:

	White	Black
1	P–Q4	N–KB3
2	P–QB4	P–QB4
3	P–Q5	P–K3
4	N–QB3	PxP
5	PxP	P–Q3

The immediate 5 ... P–KN3? would allow the paralysing thrust 6 P–Q6!

6	N–B3	P–KN3
7	B–B4	B–N2
8	Q–R4 ch	

Forcing Black to commit a piece to Q2, and thus hindering the smooth development of his Queen's side pieces.

8	...	B–Q2
9	Q–N3	Q–B2

These opening moves have figured in numerous recent games, two of which are discussed below. Let us now see what happens if White goes for the obvious win of the exchange.

10 BxP?

PLAY NOW CONTINUES:

10	...	QxB
11	QxP	Q–N3!
12	QxR	O–O

and White must either lose his Queen or allow the ruinous ... QxNP.

The games **Lutikov-Suetin**, 1959, and **Hybl-Nyman**, 1968 (postal) both continued 10 P–K4 O–O, 11 B–K2 P–QR3. Lutikov now played 12 P–QR4, and obtained only equality after 12 ... B–N5, 13 O–O QN–Q2. But Hybl's move, 12 P–K5!, throws doubt on Black's eleventh move—this game continued 12 ... N–KR4, 13 PxP Q–B1, 14 B–K3 P–QN4, 15 P–QR4 P–B5, 16 Q–R3 PxP, 17 N–Q2! with a promising position for White.

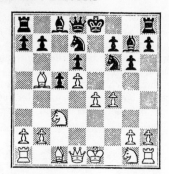

Position after 8 ... QN–Q2?

THE OPENING MOVES WERE:

	White	Black
1	P–Q4	N–KB3
2	P–QB4	P–QB4
3	P–Q5	P–K3
4	N–QB3	PxP
5	PxP	P–Q3
6	P–K4	P–KN3
7	P–KB4	B–N2
8	B–N5 ch!	

8 ...	QN–Q2?

PLAY NOW CONTINUES:

9	P–K5!	PxP
10	PxP	Q–K2
11	Q–K2	N–R4
12	P–K6	PxP
13	PxP	Q–R5 ch
14	P–KN3	NxP
15	PxN dbl ch	

The "thematic" check on QN5 can virtually win the game on its own in some variations, if Black replies incorrectly. This is the case, for example, when White already has a pawn on KB4 and is in a position to play P–K5 at once against the mistake shown in the top diagram.

The idea behind this check is to get the KB to Q3 with gain of tempo. Play normally proceeds 8 ... KN–Q2!, 9 B–Q3! (so as to answer 9 ... P–QR3 with 10 P–QR4). Black will obviously have to play his Knight back to KB3 eventually, so White has in effect had a "free" move.

This is very poor, and 8 ... B–Q2? is not much better—e.g. 9 P–K5! PxP, 10 PxP Q–K2, 11 N–KB3 and Black is completely hemmed in.

and wins.

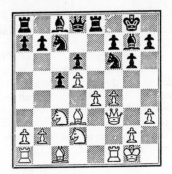

Position after 14 Q–KB3?

When Black continues correctly with 8 ... KN–Q2!, White must be very careful not to overdo the attack, as did **Taimanov** against **Trifunovic** in the USSR-Yugoslavia match, 1957: 9 B–Q3! O–O, 10 N–KB3 N–QR3, 11 O–O N–B2, 12 N–Q2 N–KB3, 13 P–KR3 R–K1, 14 Q–KB3? This move is a blunder, but Trifunovic did not notice! Play continued 14 ... R–N1?, 15 P–QR4 N–R3, 16 N–QB4 N–N5, 17 B–N1 P–QR3, 18 P–R5! B–KB1, 19 P–B5! and White won.

PLAY SHOULD HAVE CONTINUED:

14 ...	KNxQP!!
15 PxN	B–Q5 ch
16 K–R1	R–K6

winning back the piece, and remaining a pawn up.

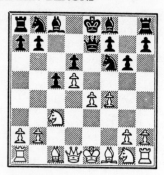

Position after 7 ... Q–K2?

P. H. Clarke's fascinating collection of brilliant short games, "Soviet Miniatures", includes a most instructive one played in the 1959 Championship of the Russian Republic. Black tries to take advantage of the multiple White pawn moves in this variation by bringing immediate pressure to bear on the KP before castling. White's combinative method of countering this system is both correct, and artistic.

THE OPENING MOVES WERE:

	Shamkovich	Zheliandinov
1	P–Q4	N–KB3
2	P–QB4	P–B4
3	P–Q5	P–K3
4	N–QB3	PxP
5	PxP	P–Q3
6	P–K4	P–KN3
7	P–B4	Q–K2?

The normal move is of course ... B–N2,

(A typical continuation is 8 P–K5!? KN–Q2!, 9 N–N5 PxP, 10 N–Q6 ch K–K2!, 11 NxB ch QxN, 12 B–B4 R–K1, 13 N–B3 K–B1 with advantage to Black.)

PLAY NOW CONTINUED:

8	N–B3!	QN–Q2?

The KP is taboo at the moment because of 9 Q–R4 ch—but Black might have been able to make a better fight of it with ... B–N2 and ... O–O, although even then his Queen would be badly misplaced on K2.

9	P–K5	PxP
10	PxP	NxKP

Now how is White to stop Black castling, with N moves dis ch hanging over his head?

11	B–N5 ch!!	

The answer is ... he just allows it.

11 ...		N(4)–Q2 dis ch
12	K–B2!	N–N5 ch
13	K–N3	N–K4
14	NxN!	QxN ch
15	B–KB4	

and Black is helpless.

The remaining moves were: 15 ... Q–B3, 16 Q–K2 ch B–K2, 17 P–Q6 P–N4, 18 B–K5 BxP, 19 BxB ch K–Q1, 20 B–B7 ch Resigns.

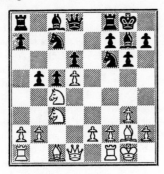

Position after 11 ... P–QN4?

When White fianchettoes his own King's Bishop, Black must beware of making the thematic advance ... P–QN4 at the wrong moment. This move is of course particularly tempting when White has just played a Knight to QB4, as in the diagrammed position.

THE OPENING MOVES WERE:

	Boleslavsky (Minsk, 1961)	**Kapengut**
1	P–Q4	N–KB3
2	P–QB4	P–QB4
3	P–Q5	P–K3
4	N–QB3	PxP
5	PxP	P–Q3
6	P–KN3	

White's aim in this variation is quick development rather than a King's side pawn rush, with the KN going swiftly to QB4.

6	...	P–KN3
7	B–N2	B–N2
8	N–KB3	O–O
9	O–O	N–R3
10	N–Q2	N–B2
11	N–QB4	

This is a tricky position for Black, and 11 ... N–K1 seems his best try. The alternative 11 ... N–KN5, 12 B–B4 N–K4 leaves White well placed after the simple 13 BxN! etc.

11	....	P–QN4?

PLAY NOW CONTINUED:

12	NxP!!	QxN
13	B–B4	Q–N3
14	P–Q6	R–Q1
15	PxN!!	RxQ
16	KRxR	

13 ... Q–Q1 is no better.

and White won easily.

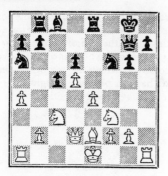

Position after 15 N–B3?

THE OPENING MOVES WERE:

	H. Keller	M. Wills
1	P–QB4	P–KN3
2	N–QB3	B–N2
3	P–Q4	P–Q3
4	P–K4	N–KB3
5	B–K2	O–O
6	P–KR4!?	

Bondarevsky's direct attack on the KR file (see page 76) was also tried out by Keller, of Switzerland, in the semi-finals of the Fifth ICCF postal championship. His opponent, M. Wills of England, failed to spot the outright refutation 9 . . . P–QN4!, and soon found himself relieved of the vital fianchettoed KB. However, even after this shrewd manoeuvre by White, Black still had a reasonable game, and an instructive position arose after 14 moves on each side.

White begins his King's side rush even earlier than Bondarevsky.

6 ...		P–B4!
7	P–Q5	P–K3
8	P–R5	

This position also arose in the postal game between **Napolitano** and **Endzelins,** in 1957 (see facing page).

8 ...		KPxP
9	BPxP	N–R3?
10	PxP	BPxP
11	B–R6!	Q–K2
12	BxB	QxB
13	Q–Q2	R–N1
14	P–R4	R–K1
15	N–B3?	

Keller-Wills actually continued 15 P–B3 N–B2, 16 N–R3 BxN, 17 RxB P–QR3, and Black eventually won on the 32nd move. Had White played 15 N–B3?, Wills had ready an interesting positional sacrifice of the exchange.

PLAY WOULD NOW HAVE CONTINUED:

15 ...		RxP!
16	NxR	NxN

15 . . . NxP? leads to grave difficulties after 16 NxN RxN, 17 N–KN5 R–Q5, 18 Q–K3 etc.
with very strong pressure.

Position after 14 O–O?

The Napolitano-Endzelins game mentioned above featured a neat tactical stroke, also involving the White KP. Napolitano played 8 PxP BxP, 9 B–B4 Q–R4, 10 Q–Q2 N–B3, 11 N–R3 N–Q5, 12 R–QN1 QR–Q1, 13 N–KN5 KR–K1, 14 O–O?

PLAY NOW CONTINUED:

14 ...	P–KR3!
15 NxB	NxP!!

and White cannot play 16 NxN because of ... QxQ, followed by ... NxB ch and ... RxN. So he must lose a pawn without compensation.

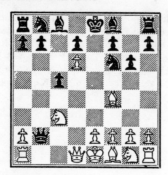

Position after 7 . . . QxNP??

It is generally agreed among theorists that 5 . . . P–Q3 is an essential preliminary to the King's side fianchetto. A possible sequel when Black fails to prevent the further advance of the White Queen's pawn was featured in the game between Kalantar and Pavlenko at Baku, 1959. The top diagram shows a simple trap set early in that game, but which remained "unsprung".

THE OPENING MOVES WERE:

	Kalantar	Pavlenko
1	P–Q4	N–KB3
2	P–QB4	P–QB4
3	P–Q5	P–K3
4	N–QB3	PxP
5	PxP	P–KN3?
6	P–Q6!	Q–N3
7	B–KB4!	QxNP??

Far too daring. Pavlenko's actual reply . . . B–N2, which is discussed on the facing page, seems the best try in a bad position.

PLAY WOULD HAVE CONTINUED:

8	B–K5!	B–N2
9	R–N1	Q–R6
10	N–N5	Q–R4 ch
11	B–B3	

forcing a decisive gain of material.

Position after 15 ... QxB

Pavlenko avoided the horrible variation mentioned above, and the game continued 7 ... B–N2, 8 Q–Q2 O–O, 9 N–B3 N–B3, 10 P–K3 R–K1, 11 B–K2 N–K5, 12 NxN RxN, 13 O–O QxNP (yielding to temptation at last ... but there is in any case little else he can do). Now White found the startling reply 14 Q–Q5!, apparently losing material, and this time the snare claimed its victim, when Black accepted the Greek gift by 14 ... RxB?, 15 PxR QxB.

PLAY NOW CONTINUED:

16	QR–K1	Q–N7
17	N–N5	Q–KB3
18	R–K8 ch	B–B1
19	RxB ch!	KxR
20	NxP ch	

and Black resigned.

Position after 10 ... QxP?

THE OPENING MOVES WERE:

Apart from watching for the special types of trap which arise in fianchetto positions, one must also keep in mind the "classic" pitfalls which are characteristic of every chess opening. For example, even in fianchetto play· it is still very poor strategy to go chasing after the opposing QNP at an early stage, as is demonstrated in this position here. The facing page exemplifies another ancient principle of play, involving the "non-existent" pin by B–N5.

Portisch	Litmanovitz
(Hungary vs Poland,	
Budapest, 1957)	
1 P–Q4	P–QB4
2 P–Q5	P–K4
3 P–K4	P–Q3
4 N–QB3	P–KN3
5 P–KB4	PxP
6 BxP	B–N2
7 N–B3	N–KB3
8 B–N5 ch	

A familiar theme in the Benoni, forcing Black to place a piece to Q2.

8 ...	B–Q2
9 B–Q3	Q–N3?
10 N–Q2!	

Exposing the weakness of Black's last move at once, since 11 N–B4 is threatened. The Queen must now decide whether to beat a humble retreat, or bite the "poison apple".

10 ...	QxP?

PLAY NOW CONTINUED:

11 N–QN5!	BxN
12 R–QN1	Q–Q5
13 BxB ch	QN–Q2
14 Q–KB3!	

and Black is hopelessly lost, in view of the threat of 15 P–B3.

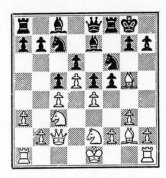

Position after 11 Q–B2?

Although it is often a good idea to play B–KN5 against a King's side fianchetto, it is rarely correct to choose the same move when the defending Bishop goes to K2 instead of KN2. The diagrammed position occurred during the game **Hoxha-Basjouni,** Prague, 1954, after the opening moves: 1 P–Q4 P–QB4, 2 P–Q5 P–K4, 3 P–QB4 P–Q3, 4 N–QB3 P–KB4, 5 P–KN3 N–KB3, 6 B–N2 B–K2, 7 P–K4 O–O, 8 KN–K2 Q–K1, 9 B–KN5? (taking pressure off K4 for the moment, but inviting trouble later) N–R3, 10 P–QR3 N–B2, 11 Q–B2?

PLAY NOW CONTINUED:

11 ...   **KNxQP!**   and Black loses a pawn for nothing.

Position after 9 . . . P–QB4?

A move which has gradually developed a question mark for itself in recent years is 9 . . . P–QB4 as an alternative to the standard 9 . . . P–KB4. This page is devoted to a study of some of the many pitfalls for Black which abound in the position after White answers the obvious 10 . . . B–KB3 with a Queen move. Of particular interest is Tal's new 11 Q–Q3!, which if anything is superior to the previously played 11 Q–B2!

THE OPENING MOVES WERE:

White	Black
1 P–Q4	N–KB3
2 P–QB4	P–K3
3 N–KB3	P–QN3
4 P–KN3	B–N2
5 B–N2	B–K2
6 O–O	O–O
7 N–B3	N–K5

Black can avoid the troubles involved in a possible P–Q5 at a later stage by simply playing 7 . . . P–Q4 here, which is quite good in spite of it blocking the diagonal.

| 8 Q–B2 | NxN |
| 9 QxN | P–QB4? |

PLAY NOW CONTINUES:

10 R–Q1!

In the first game of the **Tal-Korchnoi** match, Moscow, 1968, Tal tried 10 B–K3 instead, and Korchnoi equalised with ease by 10 . . . B–KB3, 11 KR–Q1 BxN!, 12 BxB N–B3, 13 BxN PxB, 14 Q–Q3 PxP, 15 BxP P–QB4, 16 B–B3 Q–K2.

The alternative 10 . . . P–Q3 leaves White with a strong initiative after 11 Q–B2 Q–B2, 12 P–K4!, etc.

10 . . .   B–KB3

11 Q–Q3!

Now we find Black faced with an unenviable choice of inferior alternatives—i.e. 11 . . . P–Q3?, 12 N–N5!; 11 . . . P–Q4?, 12 QPxP NPxP, 13 N–K1!; and 11 . . . Q–B1 (probably the best try), 12 P–Q5! In the third game of the 1968 Tal-Korchnoi match, Korchnoi did the best he could with 11 . . . N–QB3!?, but remained with a poor position after 12 PxP PxP, 13 QxQP Q–N3, 14 B–B4! QR–Q1, 15 Q–B7 RxR ch, 16 RxR QxP, 17 N–N5!

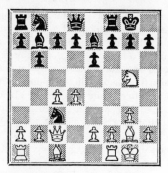

Position after 9 N–N5?

THE OPENING MOVES WERE:

	White	Black
1	P–Q4	N–KB3
2	P–QB4	P–K3
3	N–KB3	P–QN3
4	P–KN3	B–N2
5	B–N2	B–K2
6	O–O	O–O
7	N–B3	N–K5
8	Q–B2	NxN

9 N–N5?

PLAY NOW CONTINUES:

9 . . .	NxP ch!
10 QxN	BxB

No chapter on the Queen's Indian would be complete without a mention of the old chestnut where White tries to win the exchange by threatening mate on KR7 and unmasking the two fianchettoed Bishops at the same time. Indeed, it is fairly well known that Black can always occupy K5 with his Knight on the seventh move without any danger on the long diagonal. (What is not so well known though is that Black cannot play . . . P–Q4 *first*, and only then . . . N–K5. This interesting little point is dealt with on the facing page.)

Planning to strengthen K5 by . . . P–KB4 after White recaptures.

and White loses a piece for nothing.

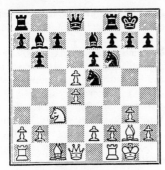

Position after 9 ... NxN?

However, Black cannot permit himself the luxury of both ... P–Q4 *and* ... N–K5. For example, after: 7 ... P–Q4, 8 N–K5! the move 8 ... N–K5? is answered by 9 PxP! NxN, 10 PxN PxP, 11 Q–B2 P–KB4, 12 B–K3 N–R3, 13 QR–B1 ± a similar result. Nor is 8 ... QN–Q2? to be recommended, because of 9 PxP PxP, 10 Q–R4!, etc. There is a pitfall concealed in the latter line, should Black be unwise enough to try and avoid the consequences of 10 Q–R4 by an immediate 9 ... NxN? (see diagram).

PLAY NOW CONTINUES:

10 P–Q6!	BxB
11 PxB	QxKP
12 PxN	BxR
13 PxN	

Or 10 ... N–B3, 11 PxB QxKP, 12 Q–R4!±

winning two pieces for Rook and pawn.

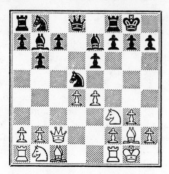

Position after 9 P–K4??

THE OPENING MOVES WERE:

	White	Black
1	P–Q4	N–KB3
2	P–QB4	P–K3
3	N–KB3	P–QN3
4	P–KN3	B–N2
5	B–N2	B–K2
6	O–O	O–O
7	Q–B2	P–Q4
8	PxP	NxP
9	P–K4??	

PLAY NOW CONTINUES:

9 ...		N–QN5!

Although generally regarded as being somewhat passive, the 7 Q–B2 line does at least prevent the counterattack ... N–K5 which is possible against 7 N–QB3. It is logical then for Black to take action in the centre with something like 7 ... P–Q4 followed by ... P–QB4 if White does nothing positive. In the diagrammed position, White has made the mistake of pushing forward too quickly with P–K4, after capturing on the eighth move.

7 ... N–K5? would be answered by 8 KN–Q2 N–Q3, 9 BxB NxB, leaving White in complete control of the centre.

The usual move 9 N–QB3 leads to equality after 9 ... P–QB4, 10 R–Q1 NxN, 11 QxN PxP, 12 RxP Q–B1.

and White must leave the KP to its fate, because 10 Q–K2 would cost the exchange after 10 ... B–QR3.

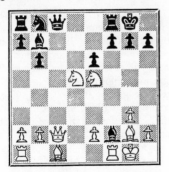

Position after 12 ... BxP ch??

At the eighth move, White can take advantage of the pinned state of Black's QP by plonking his KN on K5 to create pressure on the diagonal. Black's "book" reply is 8 ... P–QB4, with the typical continuation 9 PxBP BxP, 10 N–QB3 Q–B1, 11 PxP NxP, 12 NxN?! At first sight this looks horribly risky, since the White Queen is unguarded and in direct line with her Black counterpart. However, the obvious "win" of the Queen leads quickly to a hopeless position for Black ...

PLAY NOW CONTINUES:

13	RxB	QxQ	
14	N–K7 ch	K–R1	
15	BxB	Q–QB4	
16	BxR	QxN(4)	
17	N–B6		

and White's Rook and two Bishops will be more than a match for the Queen.

Position after 8 . . . BxN?

One gets so used to seeing White automatically fianchetto King's side, against the Queen's Indian, that it is easy to forget that development on "classic" lines can be equally good. The diagrammed position could have arisen during a game at the 1965 Zagreb tournament, if Black had been tempted to make an effort to displace the White King by means of a check at QN5.

THE OPENING MOVES WERE:

White	Black
1 P–Q4	N–KB3
2 P–QB4	P–K3
3 N–KB3	P–QN3
4 N–B3	B–N2
5 B–N5	B–K2
6 P–K3	N–K5
7 NxN	BxN
8 B–B4	

Not wishing to make Black's task easier for him by a further exchange of minor pieces. Thus far we have been following **Uhlmann-Damjanovic,** at Zagreb, but now Black was wise enough to continue in straightforward fashion with 8 . . . O–O.

(Nevertheless, Damjanovic did go strategically wrong on the ninth move—after 9 N–Q2—when he chose the retreat . . . B–N3?, leaving his Queen's side fatally weak on the White squares. The correct line, 9 . . . B–N2, was chosen by Black in Uhlmann-Padevsky, Havana, 1964 (with the previous addition of the moves . . . P–KR3, B–R4) and an equal position resulted after B–Q3 P–QB4.)

Continuing the original line, let us see what happens if Black falls for the lure of Bishop checks.

| 8 ... | BxN? |

PLAY NOW CONTINUES:

| 9 QxB | B–N5 ch |
| 10 K–Q1 | |

and Black is suddenly faced with the combined threat of both QxR, and P–B5 putting the Bishop "offside".

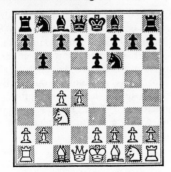

Position after 3 . . . P–QN3?

At this stage I just cannot resist slipping an ancient trap in with all the modern ones, because the finish is really out of this world. I found the line in an old magazine (no players being mentioned): 1 P–Q4 N–KB3, 2 P–QB4 P–K3, 3 N–QB3 P–QN3?, allowing White a free hand in the centre.

PLAY NOW CONTINUED:

4	P–K4!	B–N5
5	P–K5	N–K5
6	Q–N4!!	NxN
7	PxN	BxP ch
8	K–Q1	K–B1
9	R–N1	N–B3
10	B–R3 ch	K–N1
11	R–N3!	BxP
12	QxP ch	

Obviously forced.

and mate is inevitable after 13 R–N3 ch —marvellous!

Position after 9 P–Q6?

A game can be lost just as certainly through a positional blunder as through a tactical mistake which loses material. The 1963 USSR Championship at Leningrad featured an instructive error by Black in the Korchnoi-Taimanov encounter. The diagram shows the position after the optimistic 9 P–Q6? Black's next few moves paralyse White completely.

THE OPENING MOVES WERE:

	Korchnoi	Taimanov
1	P–Q4	N–KB3
2	P–QB4	P–K3
3	N–KB3	P–QN3
4	N–QB3	B–N2
5	B–KN5	

The consequences of a slightly different order of moves for White are examined on the facing page.

5	...	B–K2
6	P–K3	P–QB4!?

A daring move which invites White to try his luck with 7 P–Q5!? NxP, 8 N–K4 NxKP, 9 N–Q6 ch. However, Korchnoi elects to keep things on an even keel for the time being.

7	BxN	BxB
8	P–Q5	O–O
9	P–Q6?	

It is difficult to see what Korchnoi had in mind here, since this pawn move frees Black's position rather than cramps it.

PLAY NOW CONTINUED:

9	...	BxN ch!
10	PxB	P–KB4
11	B–K2	Q–B3

and White's position is full of weaknesses.

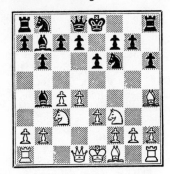

Position after 7 N–QB3?

PLAY CONTINUES:

7 . . .	P–KN4!
8 B–N3	N–K5
9 R–QB1	P–KR4
10 P–KR3	NxB

If White decides to omit the move N–QB3, he must be very careful not to leave Black with a free hand in the centre, in particular with regard to the hole on White's K4. A typical snare of this type runs as follows: 1 P–Q4 N–KB3, 2 P–QB4 P–K3, 3 N–KB3 P–QN3, 4 B–KN5 B–N2, 5 P–K3 P–KR3!, 6 B–R4 B–N5 ch!, 7 N–QB3? And now . . .

and White's pawn structure is badly disrupted.

Position after 8 B–K5?

THE OPENING MOVES WERE:

Uhlmann	O'Kelly
(Havana, 1963)	
1 P–Q4	N–KB3
2 P–QB4	P–K3
3 N–KB3	P–QN3
4 N–B3	B–N2
5 B–N5	P–KR3
6 B–R4	P–KN4
7 B–N3	N–R4

8 B–K5?

PLAY NOW CONTINUED:

8 ...	P–KB3
9 Q–B2!?	
9 ...	BxN
10 KPxB	PxB!
11 Q–N6 ch	K–K2
12 QxN	PxP

As we have seen, White is not obliged to meet Black's Queen's fianchetto with one of his own on the other side. He can proceed with purely functional development in the classic style by N–QB3 and B–KN5, etc. And in fact the German grandmaster Uhlmann was doing just that in the early Sixties, but with poorish results. A reasonable plan for Black is merely to push the Bishop away at once with ... P–KR3 and ... P–KN4, followed by ... N–KR4. If he does, White may feel tempted to move the Bishop yet again, to K5 ...

If Black doesn't care to embark on the somewhat hazardous King manoeuvre which now becomes necessary, he can simply play 7 ... B–N5, 8 P–K3 N–K5, 9 Q–B2 BxN ch, 10 PxB P–Q3 =.

When **Uhlmann** met the same line of defence against **Taimanov** the following year, also at Havana, he chose 8 Q–B2 instead, and an evenly balanced position came about after 8 ... N–QB3, 9 O–O–O NxB, 10 RPxN P–N5, 11 N–K1 Q–N4 ch!, 12 P–K3 O–O–O.

He can hardly move the Bishop back again—although it's probably the best move here!

and White was unable to retrieve his pawn after 13 N–N5 B–N2, 14 O–O–O N–B3, 15 B–Q3 P–R3, 16 N–R3 Q–K1, 17 Q–N4 Q–KB1, 18 K–N1 Q–B3.

AN EARLY B–KN5

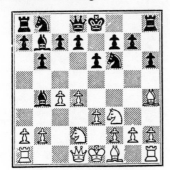

Position after 7 QN–Q2!

PLAY NOW CONTINUED:

7 ...	**P–KN4!**
8 B–N3	**P–N5**

While we are on the subject of B–KN5, readers might like to glance at what is probably the grandaddy of all Queen's Indian traps. The scene of the crime was **Tarrasch-Bogoljuboff,** Goteborg, 1920: 1 P–Q4 N–KB3, 2 P–QB4 P–K3, 3 N–KB3 P–QN3, 4 B–N5 B–N2, 5 P–K3 P–KR3, 6 B–R4 B–N5. ch, 7 QN–Q2? (KN–Q2 is the only sound move here).

and ... N–K5 wins the other Knight if the threatened one moves.

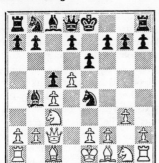

Position after 6 Q-B2?

If White tries to solve his opening problems by means of a quick King's side fianchetto (an idea first popularised by Alekhine), he must be very careful not to fall into any trap based on the consequent emergence of the Black Queen at an early stage in the game. The diagrammed position shows White playing P-KN3 on the fourth move, and then carelessly following it up with a "thematic" Q-B2 at the sixth.

THE OPENING MOVES WERE:

White	Black
1 P-Q4	N-KB3
2 P-QB4	P-K3
3 N-QB3	B-N5
4 P-KN3	P-QB4
5 P-Q5	N-K5
6 Q-B2?	

White can hold on with 6 B-Q2, although this too can be dangerous. For example, 6 B-Q2 BxN, 7 PxB? (7 BxB is the only move here) Q-B3!, etc.

PLAY NOW CONTINUES:

| 6 ... | Q-B3! |

and White must lose a pawn.

_____

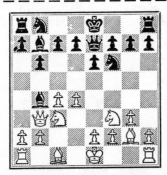

Position after 7 B-N2?

Now let's try out another early King's fianchetto for White, this time on the sixth move: 1 P-Q4 N-KB3, 2 P-QB4 P-K3, 3 N-QB3 B-N5, 4 N-B3 P-QN3, 5 Q-N3 Q-K2, 6 P-KN3. This continuation was adopted in the 1951 **Bronstein-Boleslavsky** match, and Boleslavsky now played the natural 6 ... B-N2. Bronstein replied with 7 P-QR3 BxN ch, 8 QxB. If he had instead answered the natural 6 ... B-N2 with the natural 7 B-N2?, then ...

PLAY WOULD HAVE CONTINUED:

7 ...	N-B3!
8 O-O	N-QR4
9 Q-B2	NxP

Threatening the brutal 8 ... NxP.

and White has no way of retrieving his pawn, since N-QN5 can be answered by ... P-Q4, and then ... PQR3.

Position after 8 . . . NxQBP?

The game Denker-Fine, New York, 1944, featured an interesting pawn offer by White (7 O–O) which seemed rather questionable when analysed in the months following the game—although it turned out all right for Denker on the day. Further tests in master play during the next few years seemed to confirm the theorists' verdict. But more recently the consensus of opinion has swung the other way, and the acceptance of the pawn by 7 . . . BxN and 8 . . . NxQBP seems once again to merit a question mark.

THE OPENING MOVES WERE:

	Denker	Fine
1	P–Q4	N–KB3
2	P–QB4	P–K3
3	N–QB3	B–N5
4	P–K3	P–QN3
5	B–Q3	B–N2
6	N–B3	

White may also offer a pawn here, by 6 N–K2, but this particular sacrifice is unsound.

Black is not obliged to play this line, of course—6 . . . O–O is perfectly adequate.

6	. . .	N–K5
7	O–O !	

Thus far, with minor transposition, we have the Denker-Fine game. But now Fine played 7 . . . NxN, 8 PxN BxP, which turned out badly after 9 R–QN1 B–R4, 10 B–R3 P–Q3, 11 P–B5! O–O, 12 PxQP PxP, 13 P–K4, etc.

7	. . .	BxN
8	PxB	NxQBP?

PLAY NOW CONTINUES:

9	Q–B2	BxN
10	PxB	Q–N4 ch
11	K–R1	Q–KR4
12	R–KN1	QxBP ch
13	R–N2	P–KB4

This position was at one time thought to favour Black, but numerous recent games have been won by White. Here is a typical illustration:

Taimanov-Kluger, Budapest, 1961: 14 B–N2 N–K5, 15 R–KB1 N–QB3, 16 B–K2 Q–R6, 17 P–Q5 N–R4, 18 PxP O–O–O, 19 P–K7 QR–K1, 20 P–B3 N–B4, 21 RxP KR–N1, 22 RxR RxR, 23 R–KN1 RxR ch, 24 KxR Q–R4, 25 B–B6 N–B3, 26 Q–Q1! with a won game.

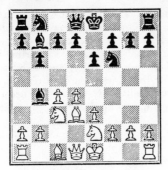

Position after 6 N–K2?

If White is unwise enough to tempt Black with the KNP at the sixth move, he soon gets into very hot water. For example, 6 N–K2?

PLAY NOW PROCEEDS:

6 ...	BxP
7 R–KN1	B–K5!
8 RxP	B–N3

followed eventually by . . . B–KB1 winning the exchange.

Another possibility is 8 BxB NxB, 9 RxP Q–B3, 10 R–N2 Q–B6, 11 K–B1 NxP!!, 12 RxN Q–R8 ch, 13 N–N1 R–KN1, regaining his piece and keeping the plus pawn.

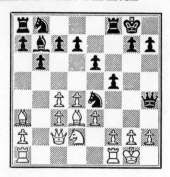

Instead of grabbing the Q BP, as in the 6 . . . N–K5 line mentioned on page 102, Black can of course choose the more discreet policy of merely supporting the Knight outpost with 7 . . . P–KB4. If White then tries to forcibly remove the intruder with 10 N–Q2 the play becomes very trappy if Black replies . . . Q–KR5.

Position after 11 B–QR3??

THE OPENING MOVES WERE:

	Aloni	**Fischer**
	(Nathanya, 1968)	
1	P–Q4	N–KB3
2	P–QB4	P–K3
3	N–QB3	B–N5
4	P–K3	P–QN3
5	B–Q3	B–N2
6	N–B3	N–K5
7	O–O	P–KB4
8	Q–B2	

(The game **Gligoric-Larsen**, Havana, 1967, continued 8 BxN PxB, 9 N–Q2 BxN, 10 PxB O–O!, 11 Q–N4 R–B4 setting a little trap, since if 12 NxP?? then . . . P–KR4 wins a piece. Gligoric didn't fall for that one, but nevertheless Black seemed already to have gained the initiative.)

8 . . .	BxN
9 PxB	O–O
10 N–Q2	Q–R5

(At this point we part company with the "parent" game, which went 11 P–B3 NxN, 12 BxN N–B3, 13 QR–K1 N–R4, 14 QR–N1 P–Q3, 15 B–K1 Q–N4, 16 Q–K2 P–K4 with equality—although Fischer eventually won.)

11 B–QR3??

PLAY WOULD NOW HAVE CONTINUED:

11 . . .	NxN	
12 QxN	BxP!!	Threatening 13 . . . Q–N5.
13 KxB	Q–N5 ch	
14 K–R1	Q–B6 ch	15 K–N1 R–B3, 16 KR moves Q–R6!, and it is all over.

If White decides to prod the Queen at the 11th turn, then Black has a surprising reply which gives him a powerful attack.

Position after 11 P–KN3

PLAY WOULD THEN CONTINUE:

11 ...   N–N4!!

and the Queen is immune from capture. Now White's King is horribly exposed, and 12 P–K4!? doesn't help one little bit because of the cheeky 12 ... PxP!

Position after 8 ... P–QN4?

When White adopts the solid Rubinstein variation at the fourth move, Black can often be tempted (even at the grandmaster level) to build into his counterplay just one too many of the various excellent motifs—all absolutely sound when used singly—which are available. In the diagrammed position, Portisch has tried to combine ... B–QN5, ... B–QN2, ... P–QB4 and ... P–QN4 all together in one glorious package.

THE OPENING MOVES WERE:

Donner	Portisch
(Wijk aan Zee, 1968)	
1 P–Q4	N–KB3
2 P–QB4	P–K3
3 N–QB3	B–N5
4 P–K3	P–QB4
5 B–Q3	O–O
6 N–KB3	P–QN3
7 P–Q5!?	

This is unusual here. White normally "goes quietly" with 7 O–O O–O, 8 B–Q2 PxP, 9 PxP P–Q4 = (Tal-Keres, Riga, 1968); or 7 B–Q2.

7 ...	B–N2
8 P–K4	P–QN4?

Black gets carried away by the sight of White's uncastled King. 8 ... P–Q3 looks strongest here.

PLAY NOW CONTINUED:

9 P–K5!	PxQBP
10 B–QN1!!	

and Black is virtually lost!

(For example: 10 ... PxP, 11 B–KN5! ±; or 10 ... BxP, 11 B–KN5 P–KR3, 12 B–R4 Q–R4, 13 PxB BxN ch, 14 PxB QxP ch, 15 Q–Q2 QxQ ch, 16 KxQ ±.)

10 ...	NxP

Portisch tried ...
and 11 BxP ch!! cost him his Queen after 11 ... KxB, 12 N–N5 ch K–N1, 13 Q–R5 QxN (12 ... K–N3 loses to 13 P–KR4! NxN, 14 Q–N4! N–K5 dis ch, 15 K–B1 NxN, 16 PxN R–R1, 17 R–R6 ch!!).

Position after 9 ... N–K5?

Even the gentle 7 B–Q2 (as played in **Gligoric-Filip,** Havana, 1967) has teeth, if Black gets the idea that he can jump straight on to K5 with impunity. For instance, a plausible continuation is 7 ... B–N2 (Filip played ... PxP, 8 PxP P–Q4!, etc.), 8 P–QR3 BxN, 9 BxB N–K5?

PLAY WOULD CONTINUE:

10	BxN	BxB
11	PxP	PxP
12	Q–Q6!	BxN	otherwise 13 Q–K5 wins.
13	PxB	Q–N3
14	Q–N3		with a very nasty attack.

Position after 8 . . . QN–Q2?

THE OPENING MOVES WERE:

If White adopts an ultra-solid set-up, and just quietly completes his development at maximum speed, Black should have little difficulty in equalising early on in the opening. Nevertheless, there are one or two little tactical points which Black must watch for. For instance, in the diagrammed position, White has just played the innocent-looking B–Q2, and Black, lulled into a sense of security, proceeds blithely on his way with a developing move.

	White	Black
1	P–Q4	N–KB3
2	P–QB4	P–K3
3	N–QB3	B–N5
4	P–K3	P–Q4
5	N–B3	O–O

As in most openings, it is wise for Black to get castled as soon as possible. Failure to do so can often have catastrophic results, even at master level. For example, here is the shortest game of the 1964 Tel-Aviv Olympics:

Uhlmann - B. Andersen: 1 P–Q4 N–KB3, 2 P–QB4 P–K3, 3 N–KB3 P–QN3, 4 N–B3 B–N5, 5 Q–B2 B–N2, 6 B–N5 P–KR3, 7 B–R4 P–Q3??, 8 Q–R4 ch N–B3, 9 P–Q5 Resigns.

6	B–Q3	P–QN3
7	O–O	B–N2
8	B–Q2	QN–Q2?

This is basically a good move, but only after 8 . . . PxP!

PLAY NOW CONTINUES:

9	NxP!!	NxN
10	PxN	BxB
11	PxP!	BxN
12	PxB	BxP
13	PxB	PxP

Otherwise he loses a pawn for nothing, and Black is positionally lost.

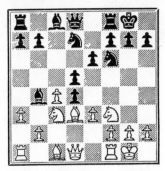

Position after 8 . . . BPxP?

Some traps of the positional type are not immediately recognised as such when they first occur, and continue to claim victim after victim until the chess world gradually begins to realise that one side is continually doing very well in the ensuing middlegame. The diagrammed position shows one of the most famous instances of this subtle kind of error. The trap is of such importance that it is included despite the fact that Black has, at the eighth move, not yet started his Queen's fianchetto.

THE OPENING MOVES WERE:

	Furman	Gipslis
	(Semi-finals of the USSR Championships, 1955)	
1	P–Q4	N–KB3
2	P–QB4	P–K3
3	N–QB3	B–N5
4	P–K3	P–B4
5	B–Q3	P–Q4
6	N–B3	O–O
7	O–O	QN–Q2
8	P–QR3	BPxP?

. . . B–R4 and . . . BxN are both reasonable at this point. But the text move leaves White with a "desperado" Knight (i.e. since he is about to be captured anyway, he may as well die gloriously!).

PLAY NOW CONTINUED:

9	QNxP!	PxN
10	PxB	PxBP
11	BxBP	N–N3
12	B–N3	PxP
13	QBxP	

and White has virtually a won game.

At least, so it appears from several master games which have featured the variation. The Furman-Gipslis continuation, and three others, are given below to show how White should handle the position from now on.

Furman-Gipslis: 13 . . . KN–Q4, 14 B–B5 R–K1, 15 R–K1 B–K3, 16 N–Q4 ±.

Korchnoi-Darga, Hastings, 1955/56: 13 . . . B–K3, 14 BxB PxB, 15 QxQ KRxQ, 16 RxP! RxR, 17 BxN R(1)–QR1, 18 BxR RxB, 19 N–K5 ±.

Tal-Tolush, USSR Championship, 1958: 13 . . . QN–Q4, 14 B–B5 R–K1, 15 R–K1 RxR ch, 16 QxR P–QN3, 17 B–Q4 B–N2, 18 R–Q1 Q–K1, 19 B–K5 ±.

Gligoric-Padevski, Olympiad, 1956: Padevski continued as Tolush until 18 . . . Q–B2, 19 B–K5 Q–K2, 20 R–Q4 R–Q1, 21 Q–Q2 ±.

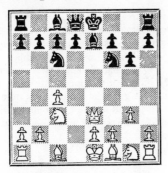

Position after 6 ... B–K2?

It is always sound for Black to start a King's fianchetto on the first move, so why shouldn't it be equally sound to do so on the second? This page gives the answer, which is ... if White can follow with a third move which obliges Black to leave his projected fianchetto for a moment, and make a centre exchange which brings the White Queen into a menacing position, then the fianchetto is indeed questionable. The diagrammed position shows an aftermath of this particular strategic blunder.

THE OPENING MOVES WERE:

Larsen	Gheorghiu
(Monaco, 1968)	
1 P–QB4	P–K4
2 P–KN3	P–KN3?
3 P–Q4!	

White hasn't exactly got a *won* game at this stage, but his prospects have certainly improved considerably since the game started two moves ago!

3 ...	PxP
4 QxP	N–KB3
5 N–QB3	N–QB3
6 Q–K3 ch	B–K2?

6 ... Q–K2 had to be tried here.

PLAY NOW CONTINUED:

7 N–Q5!	NxN

7 ... O–O is simply answered by 8 NxB ch, leaving White with a nice healthy pair of Bishops and a good grip on the centre squares.

8 PxN	N–N1

8 ... N–N5 would be answered by 9 Q–QB3!, and Black could not then play ... O–O because of 10 B–R6!, etc.

9 P–Q6!	PxP
10 N–R3	O–O
11 Q–R6	N–B3
12 N–N5!	BxN
13 BxB	P–B3
14 B–Q2	P–QN3
15 B–N2	B–N2
16 O–O	

At this point, in desperation, Gheorghiu tried to take refuge in a major piece ending with 16 ... N–R4!?, 17 BxN BxB, 18 KxB PxB, but the ruinous weakness of his pawn structure forced him to capitulate on the 38th move.

Position after 8 Q–QB4?

An interesting system, formulated by Keres, is to take advantage of White's reluctance to take up space in the centre by . . . P–QB3, as a preliminary to . . . P–Q4. This plan is best countered by N–KB3 at the appropriate moment. White can get into trouble very quickly if he decides to let the QP come forward without hindrance, and then try to capture it.

THE OPENING MOVES WERE:

	White	Black
1	P–QB4	P–K4
2	N–QB3	N–KB3
3	P–KN3	P–QB3
4	B–N2!?	

Better to hit the KP while it cannot be protected with . . . N–QB3.

(The KN can switch to the Queen's wing in the event of . . . P–K5 (after 4 N–KB3) leaving the diagonal clear for the Bishop. A game **Bagirov-Tal,** 1963, featured this line: 4 . . . P–K5, 5 N–Q4 Q–N3!?, 6 N–N3 P–QR4, 7 P–Q4?—7 N–QR4! is best here, so as to answer . . . Q–N5, with 8 N–Q4! (which incidentally sets a little trap, e.g. 8 . . . P–QN4, 9 N–B2! QxN?, 10 P–QN3 winning the Queen). Tal now continued 7 . . . P–R5, 8 P–B5 Q–N5, 9 N–Q2 P–Q4! with equality.)

Getting back to the 4 B–N2 line . . .

4 . . .	P–Q4
5 PxP	PxP
6 Q–N3!?	

Much safer is 6 P–Q3, although White has then relinquished his opening initiative.

6 . . .	N–QB3!
7 NxP	N–Q5
8 Q–QB4?	

Very tempting, but incorrect. See the facing page for the superior move 8 NxN ch.

PLAY NOW CONTINUES:

8 . . .	NxN
9 BxN	P–QN4!!

and White is at a loss for a good move. For example, 10 BxP ch K–K2, 11 Q–Q5 can be answered by . . . Q–B2!, 12 QxR KxB! with multiple threats in all directions.

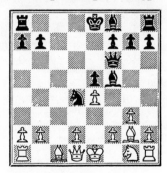

Position after 10 P–K4?

PLAY WOULD CONTINUE:

10 ...   Q–QB3!

Better for White to exchange Knights at the eighth turn, although even then his situation is fraught with difficulties. A typical instance was: 8 NxN ch QxN, 9 Q–Q3 B–KB4, 10 B–K4 B–Q2, 11 P–K3 N–K3, 12 Q–K2 N–QB4, 13 B–B2 P–K5 ∓ (**Novak-Trapl,** 1959). The alternative 9 Q–Q1 is no better, e.g. 9 ... B–KB4, 10 P–Q3 R–QB1, and White has to play the abject ... K–B1. If he tries to hit back with 10 P–K4?, then ...

and White cannot survive much longer.

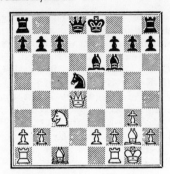

If Black feels very brave, he can try throwing forward both centre pawns to combat White's flank attack system, particularly when the game starts with 1 P–QB4. The obvious danger is that Black's "lost" tempo, as compared with similar positions with colours reversed in the Sicilian, may prove fatal in certain variations. In the play leading up to this diagram here, Black has been playing good sound "Sicilian" moves just *as if* he had castled already. But he hasn't!

Position after 10 ... B–KB3??

THE OPENING MOVES WERE:

	White	Black
1	P–QB4	P–K4
2	N–QB3	N–KB3
3	P–KN3	P–Q4
4	PxP	NxP
5	B–N2	B–K3!?

The start of a series of super-optimistic manoeuvres—5 ... N–N3 would be more circumspect.

| 6 | N–KB3 | |

Making haste slowly! 6 Q–N3!? looks good superficially, but could be adequately answered by 6 ... N–QN5!

6	...	N–QB3
7	O–O	B–K2
8	P–Q4!	

The kind of bold venture which Black would be unable to get away with in a true Dragon.

8	...	PxP
9	NxP	QNxN
10	QxN	B–KB3??

10 ... NxN was the only hope here, albeit a slim one.

PLAY NOW CONTINUES:

     11 Q–R4 ch!

and however Black plays he is either going to be skewered by the fatal pin R–Q1 (for example, 11 ... P–QB3, 12 NxN BxN, 13 R–Q1), or cut to pieces by the check on K4 (after 11 ... B–Q2, 12 Q–K4 ch N–K2, 13 QxQNP, etc.).

"DRAGON REVERSED"

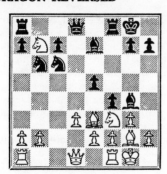

Position after 12 NxP??

PLAY NOW CONTINUES:

12 ...	Q–B1
13 B–Q2	QxN
14 NxP	P–B6!

The discreet 5 . . . N–N3 is thought to be quite sound, and White must be careful not to get too excited over his extra move. The lower diagram shows a case in point. White has just made a meal of the infamous "poisoned QNP", and now pays the usual penalty. The moves leading up to the debacle were: 5 . . . N–N3, 6 N–KB3 N–QB3, 7 O–O B–K2, 8 P–Q3 O–O, 9 B–K3 B–KN5, 10 N–K4!? P–KB4, 11 N–B5 P–B5!, 12 NxP?? (White thinks he is going to get his piece back after 13 . . . QxN with 14 NxP hitting the pinned QN—but Black has seen further!)

and White—threatened with both . . . NxN and . . . PxB—will remain a piece down.

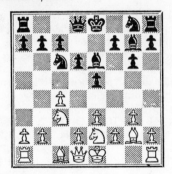

Position after 6 ... B–K3?

The game Benko-Hort, Benatky, 1969, saw White miss a very good chance at the seventh move when Black made the mistake of bringing his QB out to K3 to hit the opposing pawn on QB4. The correct answer had been known to the theorists at least as far back as the 1963/64 USA Championship, so it seems surprising that Benko (a naturalised American) was apparently unaware of the line.

THE OPENING MOVES WERE:

	Benko	Hort
1	P–QB4	P–KN3
2	P–KN3	B–N2
3	B–N2	P–K4

An excellent reply to White's system, as long as Black doesn't try for too much too soon.

4	N–QB3	N–QB3
5	P–K3	P–Q3
6	KN–K2	

Thus far **Clarke-Cafferty,** Sunderland, 1966, where Black continued 6 ... KN–K2, 7 O–O O–O with equality.

6 ...		B–K3?

Benko now chose 7 N–Q5, but was immediately pushed back by 7 ... QN–K2!, 8 P–Q4 P–QB3, 9 NxN NxN, 10 P–Q5 B–N5, 11 P–B3 B–Q2, 12 N–B3 PxP, 13 PxP P–QN4!, etc.

PLAY SHOULD NOW HAVE CONTINUED:

       7 P–Q4!

As in the game **Saidy-Addison,** USA Championship, 1963/64, which went 7 ... PxP, 8 NxP KN–K2, 9 NxB PxN, 10 O–O with advantage to White. Nor can Black improve matters with 7 ... BxP, because White regains the pawn with the better game after 8 P–Q5 BxN, 9 QxB N–N1, 10 Q–N5 ch N–Q2, 11 QxP, etc.

Position after 9 . . . N–KB4?

PLAY NOW CONTINUED:

10	P–Q5	N–K4
11	P–QN3	P–QR4
12	B–QN2	N–Q2
13	P–QR3	N–QB4
14	P–QN4	N–Q2
15	Q–N3	

Reverting to the Clarke-Cafferty continuation, it is worth noting that if White selects the aggressive 8 P–Q4, as in **Botvinnik-Reshevsky,** AVRO, 1938 (Clarke played 8 P–Q3 instead), then it is poor policy for Black to bear down directly on the White QP. For example, 8 . . . PxP, 9 PxP N–KB4?

and White's position is far superior in the centre.

The correct action to take at the ninth move was demonstrated in **Larsen-Spassky,** Belgrade, 1964: 9 . . . B–KN5!, 10 P–B3 B–KB4, 11 P–KN4 B–QB1, with a slight advantage to Black.)

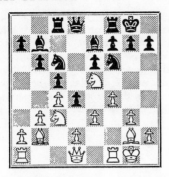

Position after 11 . . . P–Q5

The idea of advancing both Bishop's pawns in a pincer movement against the enemy centre dates back at least as far as H. E. Bird, the 19th century British player. He used it as an accessory to the Bird's Opening, with the KB going to K2. Nimzovich and Reti developed the idea further, but with a fianchetto of the KB. One of the foremost modern exponents of this "elastic centre" idea is Bent Larsen, who used it to good effect when winning the staggering total of no less than four major international tournaments in the second half of 1967.

THE OPENING MOVES WERE:

	Larsen	**Matulovic**
	(Sousse, 1967)	
1	N–KB3	P–QB4
2	P–QN3	N–KB3
3	B–N2	P–K3
4	P–B4	B–K2
5	P–N3	P–QN3
6	B–N2	B–N2
7	O–O	O–O
8	N–B3	P–Q4!?
9	N–K5	

This same position also arose in **Larsen's** games against **Pachman** and **Donner** at Havana, 1967, and **Keres** in 1967. Already White seems to have gained a strong initiative.

9	. . .	N–B3!
10	P–B4	R–B1
11	P–K3	

At this point Matulovic played 11 . . . P–QR3!, threatening to gain ground in the centre with . . . P–Q5. The immediate advance of the QP would be a serious error. For example . . .

11	. . .	P–Q5?

PLAY WOULD NOW HAVE CONTINUED:

12 N–N5!

and Black must lose the QRP—for instance 12 . . . P–QR3, 13 N–R7! NxN, 14 BxB etc,

(The game actually continued 11 . . . P–QR3!, 12 PxP PxP, 13 R–B1 P–QN4, 14 P–QR4 N–QR4, 15 PxP PxP, 16 P–QN4! breaking up the imposing facade of pawns so that White's pieces can occupy the resulting weak dark-coloured squares. The next few moves were 16 . . . PxP, 17 NxNP RxR, 18 QxR B–R3, 19 N–B6 NxN, 20 QxN Q–B1, 21 N–R7! with the advantage, since if 21 . . . Q–N2 then 22 R–R1!

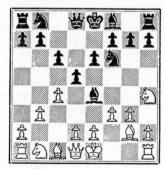

Position after 7 P–KB3??

When Black brings his QB "outside", to KB4, before setting up the pawn phalanx QB3–Q4–K3, the possibility of N–KR4 by White must always be borne in mind by both players. The two simple traps given on this page are centred around this theme. In the top diagram, White has just pushed his KBP forward to force the Bishop back to KN3, where it can be taken by the Knight (or so he thinks!).

THE OPENING MOVES WERE:

White	Black
1 N–KB3	P–Q4
2 P–QB4	P–QB3
3 P–QN3	N–KB3
4 P–KN3	B–KB4
5 B–KN2	P–K3
6 N–KR4?	B–K5
7 P–KB3??	

PLAY NOW CONTINUES:

7 . . .	BxN
8 QxB	P–KN4!

and the Knight has no retreat square.

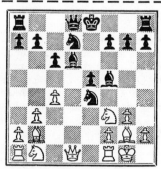

Position after 10 . . . NxKP??

But once White has got his QP on to the third rank, the Black Bishop can be chased with impunity. In this lower diagram, Black has started expanding in the centre far too quickly, and now compounds the error by gobbling up the proffered KP. The moves leading up to this debacle were: 6 B–QN2 QN–Q2, 7 O–O B–Q3, 8 P–Q3 P–K4?, 9 P–K4! PxP, 10 PxP NxKP??

PLAY NOW CONTINUES:

    10 N–KR4!   and Black must lose a piece.

(Central expansion for Black *at the right time* was demonstrated in the game **Olafsson–Tal**, Reykjavik, 1964: 1 N–KB3 P–Q4, 2 P–QB4 P–QB3, 3 P–QN3 N–KB3, 4 P–KN3 B–KB4, 5 B–KN2 P–K3, 6 B–QN2 QN–Q2, 7 O–O P–KR3, 8 P–Q3 B–K2 (this is considered by the theorists to be rather better than . . . B–Q3), 9 QN–Q2 O–O, 10 P–QR3 P–QR4, 11 B–QB3!? P–QB4!, 12 R–K1 P–Q5, 13 B–QN2 Q–B2, 14 P–KR3 P–K4 ∓.)

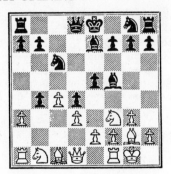

Position after 8 . . . B–KB4?

THE OPENING MOVES WERE:

The Reti can easily transpose into either a Yugoslav King's Indian Defence with a move in hand for White, or a Benoni reversed, as is discussed here. The game in question was played at the 1955 USSR Championship and Black's position became critical as early as move seven, when White gambited his QNP.

	Geller	Mikenas
1	N–KB3	P–Q4
2	P–QB4	P–Q5
3	P–KN3	P–QB4
4	B–N2	N–QB3
5	O–O	P–K4!?

Rather than continue to push pawns forward, Black should play with extreme caution (i.e. 5 . . . P–KN3) having regard to the fact that White is now playing a good sound defence *with* a move in hand.

6	P–Q3	B–K2
7	P–QN4!	PxP
8	P–QR3	

This move and the previous one are characteristic of the Wolga Gambit in the Benoni, in which Black gets pressure on the Queen's side in exchange for his pawn minus. If, knowing this, Mikenas had now tried a developing move instead of . . . PxRP, then 8 . . . B–Q2 is best here.

8 . . .	B–KB4?

PLAY WOULD HAVE CONTINUED:

9	PxP	BxNP
10	NxKP!	NxN
11	Q–R4 ch	

with a tremendous position.

Mikenas actually played 8 . . . PxRP, hoping to weather the storm, but was soon in serious difficulties after: 9 Q–R4 B–Q2, 10 BxP N–KB3, 11 Q–N5! ±.

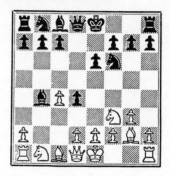

Position after 5 ... BxP??

The same move of the QNP can also be very awkward for Black if he tries to change horses in mid-stream by pushing his QP forward after first electing to protect it with ... P–K3. For example, the game **Ilivitsky-Spassky,** in the same tournament as above, started out like this: 1 N–KB3 P–Q4, 2 P–QB4 P–K3, 3 P–KN3 N–KB3, 4 B–N2 P–Q5!?, 5 P–QN4! If Spassky had now taken the QNP, retribution would have been swift.

PLAY WOULD THEN HAVE CONTINUED:

6 Q–R4 ch	N–QB3
7 N–K5!	B–Q3
8 NxN	Q–Q2
9 P–K3	

and Black is never going to get the piece back.

(Spassky chose 5 ... P–QB4 instead, but Ilivitsky maintained a strong initiative by 6 B–N2 N–QB3, 7 P–N5 N–K2, 8 P–K3! PxP, 9 QPxP QxQ ch, 10 KxQ N–N3, 11 P–KR4 P–KR3, 12 K–K2 N–KN5, 13 R–Q1 P–KB3, 14 P–QR4 B–Q2, 15 KN–Q2 O–O–O, 16 N–N3 N(3)–K4, 17 N–R3, etc.)

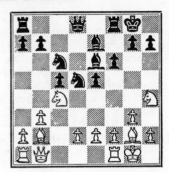

Position after 11 ... B–K3?

When White brings his QN round via QR3 to recapture on QB4, the resulting positions can take on a marked resemblance to the Maroczy Bind variation of the Sicilian Defence, but with colours reversed. In the diagrammed position Black has strengthened his centre with ... P–KB3, as White would do in the Sicilian, and now proceeds blithely on his way with the "good" strategical move 11 ... B–K3?, overlooking a tactical "change of direction" which is available to White.

THE OPENING MOVES WERE:

White	Black
1 N–KB3	P–Q4
2 P–QB4	PxP
3 N–QR3	P–QB4
4 NxP	N–QB3
5 P–QN3	P–K4?!
6 B–N2	P–KB3
7 P–KN3	KN–K2
8 B–N2	N–Q4

Now the Black KN has reached exactly the same square as White's KN does in the Sicilian, and is flanked by the characteristic "Bind" pawns.

9 O–O	B–K2
10 N–KR4!	

A signal that White has ambitions on the King's side—but Black ignores the danger.

10 ...	O–O
11 Q–N1	

A fierce attacking move made on the back row—a common theme in the modern chess opening.

11 ...	B–K3?

PLAY NOW CONTINUES:

12 B–K4!	

Suddenly the fianchettoed Bishop is menacing the King's side!
12 ... P–KR3 fails to 13 B–R7 ch K–R1, 14 N–N6 ch, etc.

12 ...	P–KN3
13 BxKNP!	PxB
14 QxP ch	K–R1
15 Q–R6 ch	K–N1
16 N–N6	

and Black is in a horrible mess.

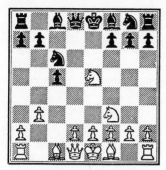

Position after 6 QNxP??

Grabbing the KP at move 6 is very poor tactics—poor strategy as well, since a fianchetto once started should be completed as soon as possible.

PLAY WOULD NOW CONTINUE:

6 . . .	NxN
7 NxN	Q–Q5!

and both Knight and Rook are out on a limb. White can only protect one at a time, so a piece is lost.

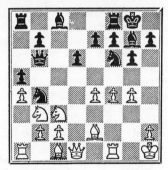

Position after 13 P–KN4!?

At the time of writing, the 4 P–B4 and 6 B–K2 system against the Pirc is under something of a cloud, owing principally to the game mentioned below. When Fischer went down to Korchnoi at Curacao 1962, most of the world's master players turned immediately to other methods of attack for White. However, as is pointed out on the following page, the system is quite good up to the ninth move, and deserves a return to popularity.

THE OPENING MOVES WERE:

	Fischer	Korchnoi
1	P–K4	P–Q3
2	P–Q4	N–KB3
3	N–QB3	P–KN3
4	P–B4	B–N2
5	N–B3	O–O
6	B–K2	P–B4

6 ... P–B3 is quite playable here, although rarely seen in practice.

7	PxP	Q–R4
8	O–O	QxP ch
9	K–R1	N–B3
10	N–Q2	P–QR4
11	N–N3	Q–N3
12	P–QR4	N–QN5!

This is a very difficult position for White, although not a losing one. For instance, 13 B–B3 can be answered by B–K3!, 14 N–Q5 KNxN! and 15 ... B–B4! Nor does the immediate 13 N–Q5 help, because of KNxN, 14 PxN B–B4!, etc. The thrust 13 P–B5 is probably best, although somewhat risky.

13 P–KN4!?

Another little trap here is 13 R–KB3? N–KN5!, winning a pawn (**Spurgeon-Howson,** 1968).

PLAY NOW CONTINUED:

| 13 ... | BxP! | and White's position is shattered. |

But Fischer did the best he could, and Korchnoi had to find a tremendous twentieth move to clinch victory. The game continued: 14 BxB NxB, 15 QxN NxP, 16 N–N5 NxR, 17 NxN Q–B3, 18 P–B5 Q–B5, 19 Q–B3 QxRP, 20 N–B7 QR–K1!!, 21 N–Q5 QxN, 22 B–N5 QxP, 23 BxP B–K4, 24 R–B2 Q–B8 ch, 25 R–B1 Q–R3, 26 P–R3 PxP, 27 BxR RxB, 28 N–K7 ch K–R1, 29 NxP Q–K3!, 30 R–KN1 P–R5, 31 R–N4 Q–N6, 32 Q–B1 P–R6, 33 R–N3 QxR, 34 Resigns, since ... P–R7 wins.

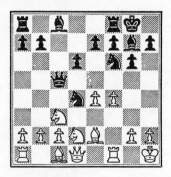

Position after 10 ... N–Q5?

THE OPENING MOVES WERE:

In the same year (1962) that Fischer lost to Korchnoi with 13 P–KN4?, another game of great theoretical interest was played in the British Championship at Whitby, between **Hindle** and **Penrose**. Hindle chose what is probably the best possible 13th move, P–B5, and was able to keep his end up with 13 ... P–Q4, 14 P–K5 N–K5, 15 NxN PxN, 16 PxP RPxP, 17 B–QB4, etc (although he eventually lost). This page is concerned with emphasising the tremendous importance of 10 ... P–QR4 for Black, and shows how the tempting alternative 10 ... N–Q5? should be handled.

Liberzon	Kudinov

(This game, from the Moscow vs Leningrad match 1958, seems to be the "grandaddy" of the whole variation.)

1	P–K4	P–Q3
2	P–Q4	N–KB3
3	N–QB3	P–KN3
4	P–B4	B–N2

Penrose actually played these first four moves the other way round, leaving ... N–KB3 to last, doubtless to avoid a possible 4 B–KN5!

5	N–B3	O–O
6	B–K2	P–B4
7	PxP	Q–R4
8	O–O	QxP ch
9	K–R1	N–B3
10	N–Q2	

Now we part company with both Penrose and Korchnoi, both of whom selected the powerful 10 ... P–QR4.

10	...	N–Q5?

PLAY NOW CONTINUED:

11	N–N3	NxN
12	RPxN	P–QN4!?

Obviously intending to answer 13 BxP with ... NxP!, etc.

13	P–K5!	PxP
14	PxP	N–K1

(**Nikitin-Bondarevsky**, Moscow, 1958, continued 14 ... QxP, 15 B–KB4 Q–QB4, 16 B–B3 B–B4, 17 BxR RxB, 18 Q–B3 R–QB1, 19 B–K3 with a won game.)

15	P–QN4!	Q–N3
16	B–KN5	

with a tremendous advantage.

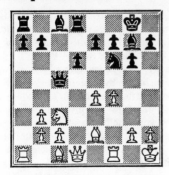

Position after 12 ... R–Q1?

The alternative 12 ... R–Q1? was featured in the game **Henriksen-Watzl,** Danish Correspondence Championship, 1961.

PLAY NOW CONTINUED:

13 P–K5!	N–K1
14 B–K3!!	Q–B2
15 B–N6!	

14 ... QxB leaves the Queen trapped after 15 N–Q5! Q–B4, 16 P–QN4 or 15 ... Q–K5, 16 B–B3.
winning the exchange at least since the Queen is lost after 15 ... QxB?, 16 N–Q5!

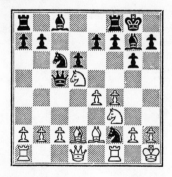

Position after 11 . . . N–B7 ch??

THE OPENING MOVES WERE:

One rather obvious trap which is in danger of being completely forgotten, owing to the current popularity of the 10 N–Q2 line, is where White tries instead 10 B–Q2, inviting Black to "win" the exchange by Knight checks on KB7. The drastic punishment which awaits this course of action is shown below. However, the variations starting with 10 . . . N–KN5!? are not without danger for White also, as is discussed on the facing page.

	White	Black
1	P–K4	P–Q3
2	P–Q4	N–KB3
3	N–QB3	P–KN3
4	P–KB4	

The Austrian Attack.

4	. . .	B–N2
5	N–KB3	O–O
6	B–K2	P–QB4
7	PxP	Q–R4
8	O–O	QxP ch
9	K–R1	N–QB3
10	B–Q2	

With the nasty threat of N–QR4 in some variations (e.g. 10 . . . P–K4??, 11 N–QR4! wins the Queen!).

10 . . . P–QN4 seems best here.

10	. . .	N–KN5!?
11	N–Q5!	N–B7 ch??

PLAY NOW CONTINUES:

12	RxN	QxR
13	B–K3!	

and the Queen is trapped.

Position after 12 ... BxR?

That much is easy to see. But if Black tries instead 11 ... BxP, then play becomes very complicated indeed (readers in search of further information should consult the May 1965 issue of the BCCS Newsletter). One typical snare must suffice here for the purposes of illustration: 12 P–KR3!! (otherwise Black will merely retire his KB and remain a pawn up) BxR? (see diagram).

PLAY NOW CONTINUES:

13 QxB	N–B7 ch
14 RxN!	QxR
15 NxP ch!!	
15 ...	NxN
16 Q–B6!!	

Who could hope to find all these glorious moves in practical play?

and the combined threats of P–B5 and B–B3 are unanswerable. Black's best twelfth move seems to be the humble ... N–R3, leaving White with a strong initiative.

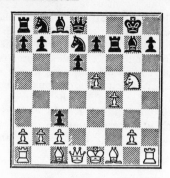

Position after 11 N–N5?

One of the wildest lines in the Pirc is where Black deliberately invites a pawn storm on the King's side by answering 6 P–K5 with the provocative . . . KN–Q2. White can then drive his RP right into the heart of the Black stronghold, ignoring the annihilation of his QN on the opposite wing. G. S. Botterill has done a great deal of work on the resulting positions, and Pirc addicts are recommended to study his articles on the subject in *Chessman Quarterly*. In the diagrammed position, White has continued the attack incorrectly.

THE OPENING MOVES WERE:

> **Bykhovsky   Bebchuk**
> (Moscow Team Championship, 1966)
>
> | | | |
> |---|---|---|
> | 1 | P–K4 | P–Q3 |
> | 2 | P–Q4 | N–KB3 |
> | 3 | N–QB3 | P–KN3 |
> | 4 | P–B4 | B–N2 |
> | 5 | N–B3 | O–O |
> | 6 | P–K5 | KN–Q2 |
> | 7 | P–KR4!? | |

White can of course continue in more restrained fashion with 7 B–B4.

> | | | |
> |---|---|---|
> | 7 | . . . | P–QB4! |
> | 8 | P–R5 | BPxP |
> | 9 | RPxP!? | |

Here again White can restrict his intended material loss merely to pawns by 9 QxP PxKP, 10 Q–B2 (or N1).

> | | | |
> |---|---|---|
> | 9 | . . . | PxN |
> | 10 | PxBP ch | RxP |
> | 11 | N–N5? | |

11 B–B4 is best here.

PLAY NOW CONTINUED:

> | | | |
> |---|---|---|
> | 11 | . . . | PxNP! |
> | 12 | B–B4 | |
> | 12 | . . . | NxP!! |

12 BxNP fails to . . . Q–R4 ch. and White is lost in all variations.

(Bykhovsky—realising that both PxN and NxR are easily refuted by . . . Q–R4 ch —tried 13 Q–R5, but was unable to avoid ruinous material deficit after 13 . . . Q–R4 ch, 14 K–B1 P–Q4!, etc.)

Position after 12 ... NxKP?

The recent correspondence game **Sorokin-Dubovik** (both of the USSR) showed that even White's best move, 11 B–B4, is suspect against Dubovik's innovation 11 ... P–K3! (... N–B1 was previously considered strongest). White seems to have nothing better than 12 N–N5 N–B1, 13 NxR KxN, 14 P–B5 PxNP, 15 PxP ch BxP, 16 R–B1 ch K–N1, 17 RxN ch KxR, 18 Q–B3 ch Q–B3!, etc. (**Demichev-Seredenko**, Kazakhstan, 1966). Dubovik actually played 12 ... NxKP?

PLAY NOW CONTINUED:

13	PxN	Q–R4
14	Q–R5!	QxP ch
15	B–K2	R–B4
16	P–KN4	PxP
17	PxR	Q–R4 ch
18	K–Q1	Q–Q4 ch
19	B–Q3	QxR ch
20	QxQ	PxR = Q
21	Q–R5!	Q–B3
22	PxP	N–B3
23	P–K7!	NxP
24	B–QN2!	

and wins.

Position after 10 B-B4?

An idea introduced by **Bronstein** (against **Vasyukov** in the 1965 USSR Championship, at Tallinn) is to recapture with the QP if Black exchanges pawns in answer to 6 P-K5. Bronstein achieved a fine position when Vasyukov continued with . . . QxQ ch, . . . R-Q1 ch and . . . N-Q4. But Black can also try 9 . . . N-K1, as I did against Hartston in the 1967 Cambridgeshire vs Essex match. White must then take care with the exact order of his developing moves.

THE OPENING MOVES WERE:

	Hartston	Howson
1	P-K4	P-Q3
2	P-Q4	N-KB3
3	N-QB3	P-KN3
4	P-KB4	B-N2
5	N-KB3	O-O
6	P-K5	PxP
7	QPxP	

7 BPxP gives Black an easy game after the obvious . . . N-Q4.

7	. . .	QxQ ch
8	KxQ!	R-Q1 ch
9	K-K1	

The alternative 9 B-Q3 is discussed on the facing page.

| 9 | . . . | N-K1! |

Vasyukov played . . . N-Q4 here, and Bronstein maintained a strong initiative by 10 NxN RxN, 11 B-B4 R-Q1, 12 N-N5 P-K3, 13 B-K3, etc.

| 10 | B-B4? | |

No doubt with the idea of gambitting the QBP—but Black is in no hurry to take it.

PLAY NOW CONTINUED:

| 10 | . . . | B-B4 |
| 11 | B-K3 | N-QB3! |

As expected.

threatening . . . N-N5, *and* cutting out N-Q4 (which would have been a good reply to BxBP).

White now had to resort to anti-positional moves to save his pawn, and Black broke open the centre to the acute embarrassment of the Black King: 12 R-QB1 N-R4, 13 B-K2 P-KB3, 14 K-B2 N-QB3, 15 PxP KBxP, 16 P-KR3 N-Q3, and Black won on the 29th move (although possibly White can hold this position with absolutely correct defence).

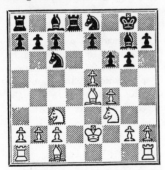

Position after 11 1 .. P–KB3?

PLAY NOW CONTINUED:

12	B–Q5 ch!	K–R1
13	BxN	PxB
14	P–KR3!	B–B4?
15	P–KN4!	B–K3
16	B–K3	

The game **Roe-Howson,** Southend, 1969, continued 9 B–Q3 N–K1, 10 K–K2 N–QB3, 11 B–K4. Now Black—remembering "with advantages" (as the Bard has it) his great deeds on the field of Cambridge—played 11 ... P–KB3? (11 ... B–B4 is better).

An additional blunder which turns a bad game into a lost one.

Realising too late that ... BxBP loses a piece after N–K1!

and Black's horrible pawn formation proved his downfall after a lengthy and positively agonising endgame.

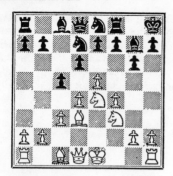

Position after 9 ... K–R1?

White can avoid the pitfalls of the very well analysed 6 B–K2 lines by playing 6 B–Q3 instead, in which case it will be Black's turn to tread carefully. His best reply is ... QN–Q2, threatening ... P–K4, which White should answer with P–K5, initiating a King's side attack which needs very careful handling.

THE OPENING MOVES WERE:

Kogan   **Schoydun**
(Correspondence game, 1963/64)

1	P–K4	P–Q3
2	P–Q4	N–KB3
3	N–QB3	P–KN3
4	P–B4	B–N2
5	N–B3	O–O
6	B–Q3	QN–Q2
7	P–K5!	

7 O–O allows Black to equalise easily by ... P–K4!, 8 BPxP PxP, 9 PxP (Fischer has experimented with P–Q5 here) QNxP!, 10 NxN Q–Q5 ch, etc.

7 ...	N–K1
8 N–K4	

(An interesting possibility here is 8 P–K6!? PxP, 9 P–KR4 P–QB4, 10 P–R5! PxQP, 11 N–K4 P–Q4!, 12 N(4)–N5 R–B3, 13 PxP PxP, 14 N–R7 N–B1!, 15 NxR ch PxP, 16 NxP P–K4, 17 N–KB3! Q–Q3!, as in **Yerbury–Howson,** 1968, which was eventually drawn.)

8 ...	P–QB4
9 P–B3	K–R1?

Doubtless hoping to play ... P–KB3 without having to worry about Bishop checks. 9 ... Q–N3 is probably best.

PLAY NOW CONTINUED:

10 P–KR4	N–B2
11 P–R5	P–B5
12 B–B2	K–N1

Admitting the error of his ways.

Kogan now finished the job in great style: 13 RPxP RPxP, 14 Q–K2 P–Q4, 15 N(4)–N5 P–KB4, 16 P–KN4! Q–K1, 17 Q–R2 N–B3 (what else?), 18 PxN PxP dis ch, 19 N–K5! Resigns.

Another sparkling attack by White was conducted by **Tate** in his game against **Davies** at Whitby, 1964. The crucial point came at the 13th turn, after the moves 8 P–KR4!? P–QB4, 9 P–R5 BPxP, 10 RPxP RPxP, 11 P–K6!? PxN, 12 PxP ch RxP, 13 N–N5. Now Black lost his nerve and played the over-aggressive 13 . . . PxP?, whereas the defensive . . . P–K3!, 14 BxP R–B3 might well have salvaged a draw from the wreckage.

PLAY NOW CONTINUED:

14 KBxP!	PxR = Q
15 B–R7 ch	

and mate next move.

Position after 6 . . . B–KN5?

One defensive possibility for Black that can certainly be consigned to the dustbin is 6 . . . B–KN5? Although no absolutely immediate tactical refutation can be laid down, the fact remains that White has won numerous games against the line at the master level in recent years. Here are three examples from the last decade, all won convincingly by the White pieces.

THE OPENING MOVES WERE:

	White	Black
1	P–K4	P–Q3
2	P–Q4	N–KB3
3	N–QB3	P–KN3
4	P–B4	B–N2
5	N–B3	O–O
6	B–Q3	B–KN5?

See page 134 for the sound reply 6 . . . QN–Q2. Another move which has stood the test of time is . . . N–QB3, with the idea of chasing the B on Q3 if White plays P–Q5. In addition, there is the rather peculiar 6 . . . N–R3!?

PLAY NOW CONTINUES:

7	P–KR3	BxN
8	QxB	

These moves were common to all three games now mentioned, the first two continuing 8 . . . N–QB3:

Fischer-Benko, USA Championship, 1963: 9 B–K3 P–K4, 10 QPxP PxP, 11 P–B5 PxP, 12 QxP N–Q5, 13 Q–B2 N–K1, 14 O–O N–Q3, 15 Q–N3 K–R1, 16 Q–N4 P–QB3, 17 QR–B5 Q–K1, 18 BxN PxB, 19 R–B6!! K–N1, 20 P–K5 P–KR3, 21 N–K2 and Black resigned. **Penrose-Robatsch,** Hastings, 1961/62: 9 B–K3 N–Q2, 10 Q–B2 N–N5, 11 B–QB4 N–N3, 12 B–N3 N–QB3, 13 O–O N–R4, 14 QR–Q1 N(3)–B5, 15 B–B1 P–QB3, 16 P–B5 Q–B2, 17 R–Q3 P–QN4, 18 R–B3 with considerable advantage to White.

The third game featured 8 . . . P–K4:

Korchnoi-Robatsch, 1963: 9 QPxP PxP, 10 P–B5 N–QB3, 11 B–KN5 N–Q5, 12 Q–B2 P–QR3, 13 Q–R4 P–QB4, 14 O–O Q–N3, 15 R–B2 QR–QB1, 16 QR–KB1 PxP, 17 PxP P–B5, 18 N–K4! NxN, 19 P–B6 Resigns.

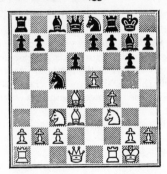

Position after 10 ... N-QB4?

PLAY WOULD NOW CONTINUE:

	Gligoric	Larsen
11	BxKNP	N-K3
12	B-K4	NxP
13	BxP ch!	KxB
14	N-N5 ch	K-N3
15	RxN	KxN
16	B-K3	

The bizarre alternative 6 ... N-R3!? was tried out in grandmaster play by (typically!) Larsen against Gligoric, at Beverwijk, 1967. Larsen got into difficulties after 7 O-O P-B4, 8 P-Q5 N-B2, 9 Q-K1?! (but won anyway on the 45th move). If White plays instead 7 P-K5! N-K1, 8 O-O P-QB4, 9 B-K3 BPxP, 10 BxQP there is a neat little trap into which Black may fall by 10 ... N-QB4? (thinking it will be OK to answer 11 BxKNP—which threatens BxN— with ... N-K3 and ... NxKBP).

with a mating attack.

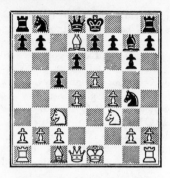

Position after 8 BxB ch?

Black is not absolutely obliged to castle before striking back, with ... P–QB4, against the Austrian Attack. The top diagram shows a position from **Purdy-R. Byrne,** played in America during 1967. White has checked on QN5, and followed with the correct P–K5, but now he tries to dodge the minefield of complications implicit in the right move 8 P–K6, and substitutes the weak 8 BxB ch?

THE OPENING MOVES WERE:

	Purdy	R. Byrne
1	P–K4	P–Q3
2	P–Q4	N–KB3
3	N–QB3	P–KN3
4	P–KB4	B–N2
5	N–KB3	P–QB4
6	B–N5 ch	B–Q2
7	P–K5	N–N5
8	BxB ch?	

PLAY NOW CONTINUED:

8	...	QxB

Now White realises that his centre is about to crumble away into nothing, so he launches out into an unsound combination based on the supposition that Black will find 10 P–K6 difficult to handle.

9	N–KN5	PxQP!

But Byrne has seen further into the position, and merely ignores the "threat".

10	P–K6	PxKP
11	QxN	PxN
12	NxKP	PxP!
13	NxB ch	K–B2

Doubtless a horrible shock for Purdy.

Now Black has no less than four pieces en prise, and cannot avoid losing two of them, thus emerging from the fray a clear piece down. The remaining moves were: 14 QxQ PxB = Q ch (the heroic pawn dies gloriously at last, in the heart of the White stronghold), 15 RxQ NxQ, 16 R–QN1 N–QB4, 17 Resigns.

Position after 10 N–KN5?

In the normal continuation, after 8 P–K6 BxB, 9 PxP ch K–Q2!, White may feel tempted (as he did above) to try the move N–KN5 instead of the recommended NxB. This variation featured in the game **Jensen-Keene,** The Hague, 1967, and was soon shown to be inferior.

PLAY NOW CONTINUED:

10 ...	P–KR4
11 NxB	Q–R4 ch
12 N–QB3	PxP
13 Q–K2	PxN
14 Q–K6 ch	K–Q1
15 P–N4	

Obviously the move Jensen was relying on (and indeed Keene was induced at the time to play defensively with 15 ... Q–N3, 16 R–B1 N–KB3—winning anyway on the 28th move). However, as was later pointed out, it should lead to a forced loss at once by 15 ... Q–N3, 16 R–B1 N–QB3!, 17 QxNP NxNP, 18 QxB NxP ch, 19 K–Q1 N(7)–K6 ch, 20 BxN QxB, 21 QxR ch K–Q2, etc.

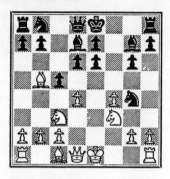

Position after 8 ... PxKP?

If Black does launch the immediate counterattack ... P–QB4, he must be prepared to have his King chivvied to and fro in the centre if White selects the sharpest possible continuation. Great accuracy in defence is required if the attack is to be successfully parried.

THE OPENING MOVES WERE:

	White	Black
1	P–K4	P–Q3
2	P–Q4	N–KB3
3	N–QB3	P–KN3
4	P–B4	B–N2
5	N–B3	P–B4

Recent analysis seems to prove that the alternative 5 ... O–O is so strong that this move is hardly worth trying, sound though it is.

| 6 | B–N5 ch | B–Q2 |

This seems the best reply. Both 6 ... KN–Q2 and 6 ... K–B1 have been played here, with poor results for Black.

| 7 | P–K5 | N–N5 |
| 8 | P–K6 | PxKP? |

The only good move is 8 ... BxB, leading to plenty of fresh air for the black King after 9 PxP ch K–Q2! (9 ... KxP? loses to 10 N–N5 ch and 11 NxB, etc.), 10 NxB Q–R4 ch, 11 N–B3 PxP, 12 NxP.

PLAY NOW CONTINUES:

9 N–N5!   and the threat of NxKP is unanswerable.

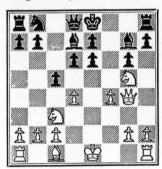

Position after 10 ... PxKP?

PLAY NOW CONTINUES:

11 NxRP!

The same trap exists in a slightly different setting if White tries to upset Black with an immediate 8 N–N5 (instead of 8 P–K6), as in **Lee-Suttles,** Havana, 1966. In this case Black should take the Bishop right away, and then return to Q2 after 9 QxN. If White makes the obvious reply, 10 P–K6, Black must continue 10 ... QBxP!, 11 NxB PxN, 12 PxP BxN ch, 13 PxB Q–R4!, etc. Capturing with the KBP instead is a serious error ...

forcing Black to give up the exchange.

Position after 3 P–KN3?

White's idea, when choosing a Kings' fianchetto as early as the third move, is to eventually force Black into one of the main lines of the King's Indian Defence. But even at the third turn there exists a strategic pitfall for White. In the diagrammed position Rycke has played the first three moves in the wrong order, and O'Kelly takes the initiative without further ado.

THE OPENING MOVES WERE:

Rycke	O'Kelly
(Brussels, 1957)	
1 P–K4	P–KN3
2 P–Q4	B–N2
3 P–KN3?	

3 N–QB3 is perfectly OK here of course, but if White hopes for a possible transposition into the King's Indian he must try 3 P–QB4 now.

PLAY NOW CONTINUED:

3 ... P–Q4!

This fine stroke leaves White poised between the tactical "devil" 4 PxP and the strategic "deep blue sea" 4 P–K5, and he selects the latter.

(It is interesting to note that 3 ... P–Q4! is also the best way to counter an attempt by White to set up a line of pawns across the centre backed up by P–QB3. I tried this plan against **Keene** at the 1967 Ilford tournament: 1 P–K4 P–KN3, 2 P–Q4 B–N2, 3 P–QB3 (hoping to be permitted the luxury of 4 P–KB4) P–Q4!, 4 PxP QxP, 5 N–KB3 N–KB3, 6 B–K2 O–O, 7 O–O P–QB4!, and Black is well placed—although I eventually escaped with a draw at the 32nd move.)

Now back to Rycke-O'Kelly ...

4 P–K5	P–QB4
5 P–QB3	N–QB3
6 B–N2	N–R3
7 N–B3	Q–N3

and Black was obliged to give up control of the centre by 8 PxP QxBP, leaving Black with almost a won game.

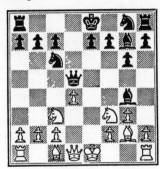

Position after 7 N–B3?

Reverting to a discussion of the tactical "devil", let us see how White gets on if he simply takes the annoying QP: 4 PxP QxP, 5 N–KB3 B–N5, 6 B–N2 N–QB3, and the pressure on White's centre will soon become unbearable. And if he tries to push the Queen away with 7 N–B3?, then . . .

PLAY WILL CONTINUE:

7 . . .	Q–K3 ch
8 B–K3	NxP!

winning a pawn.

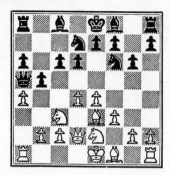

Position after 8 ... P–QN4?

When White trains his guns on KR6 right from the start, it is very often good policy for Black not to castle King's side at all, but to commence operations on the Queen's side with the King still at K1. This is an effective strategy, but needs careful handling tactically, particularly if the Queen is involved at the "front line". The square QN5 is a particularly dangerous one for her majesty in many variations.

THE OPENING MOVES WERE:

Kurajica   **G. A. Hollis**
(Islington, 1968)

1	P–K4	P–Q3
2	P–Q4	N–KB3
3	N–QB3	P–KN3
4	P–B3	P–B3!

One good P–B3 deserves another! Black intends to leave his KB on B1.

5	B–K3	QN–Q2
6	P–QR4!	

Considerably reducing Black's counter-chances on the wing.

6	...	Q–R4
7	Q–Q2	P–QR3
8	KN–K2	

This "wait-and-see" attitude pays off at once when Black rushes precipitously forward on the Queen's side.

8 ... P–KR4 and 8 ... R–QN1 were both quite playable here.

8	...	P–QN4?

PLAY NOW CONTINUED:

9	P–QN4!	

Winning a pawn at least, since 9 ... Q–N3 would be answered by 10 P–Q5 Q–N2, 11 PxQBP QxP, 12 PxP PxP, 13 RxR QxR, 14 NxP.

Venturing onto the fatal square—but there is nothing better.

9	...	QxNP
10	PxP	BPxP
11	N–B4!	B–QN2
12	N–Q3	Q–B5
13	N–B5	

and Black must lose either a piece for nothing, or Queen for two minor pieces.

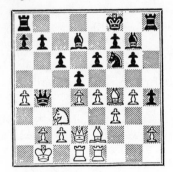

Position after 18 ... Q–N5?

The square QN5 also proved fatal for the Black Queen in the game between **Sanguinetti** and **Schweber,** at the 1965 Argentine Championship. The diagrammed position arose after White's 18th move P–KN4, and Black plunged into the pit with 18 ... Q–N5? (the opening moves are given below).

PLAY NOW CONTINUED:

19	NxP!	NxN

19 ... QxQ fails against the Zwischenzug 20 B–Q6 ch.

20	QxQ	NxQ
21	B–Q6 ch	

and 22 BxN, winning a pawn.

Sanguinetti–Schweber: 1 P–K4 P–Q3, 2 P–Q4 N–KB3, 3 N–QB3 P–KN3, 4 P–B3 P–B3, 5 B–K3 B–N2!?, 6 Q–Q2 QN–Q2, 7 KN–K2 P–KR4!, 8 P–QR4 Q–R4, 9 N–B1 P–R5, 10 B–K2 N–B1, 11 N–N3 Q–B2, 12 O–O–O P–Q4, 13 N–B5 P–K3, 14 K–N1 N(1)–Q2, 15 B–KB4 Q–N3, 16 NxN BxN, 17 KR–K1 K–B1, 18 P–KN4.

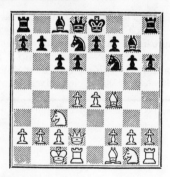

Position after 7 ... QN–Q2?

THE OPENING MOVES WERE:

	Fischer	Mednis
1	P–K4	P–Q3
2	P–Q4	N–KB3
3	N–QB3	P–KN3
4	B–KN5	B–N2
5	Q–Q2	P–KR3
6	B–KB4	P–B3
7	O–O–O	QN–Q2?

Possibly the strongest line of all for White is where the Queen's Bishop is played out to N5 on the fourth move, with the idea of getting castled Queen's side as soon as possible, thus clearing the lines for a crushing King's side attack. The game discussed here is from the 1957/58 US Championship, when the 14(!)-year-old Bobby Fischer astonished the chess world by winning the title well ahead of a very strong field which included the great Reshevsky himself.

I believe Black's best plan here is either ... P–KR3 (see page 148), or the immediate ... P–B3, waiting to see whether White plays 5 Q–Q2, in which case 5 ... P–QN4! starts a counter-attack at once.

Otherwise White will simply play B–KR6 and seriously weaken Black's King's side defences.

The game actually continued as shown on the facing page, but it is well worth noting at this stage that this sort of move by the QN often leads to a fatal weakening of the pawn structure, as shown below.

PLAY COULD THEN CONTINUE:

8	P–K5!	PxP
9	PxP	N–R4
10	P–K6!	PxP
11	B–Q3	

and White must surely win the game very shortly.

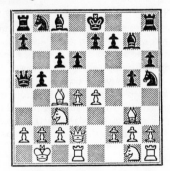

Position after 10 . . . P–QN4?

Mednis played the much better move 7 . . . Q–R4, and the game continued 8 K–N1 P–KN4, 9 B–N3 N–R4, 10 B–QB4. This provoked the obvious, and unsound, reply 10 . . . P–QN4? (see diagram). A flank advance of this kind is often Black's only chance of counterplay in the Pirc, but the consequent weakening of the long diagonal should always be taken carefully into account.

PLAY SHOULD NOW HAVE CONTINUED:

11 NxP!

and Black could not have captured the Knight because of B–Q5, etc. Most uncharacteristically, Fischer failed to spot the blunder, and moved his Bishop back to QN3 (winning the game eventually anyway).

Position after 7 P–K5?

If White tries to rush Black off his feet in the first half-dozen or so moves, with a quick B–KN5 and P–K5, he will always get the worst of it if Black plays accurately. However, the correct defensive moves would be very hard to find in actual play, and should therefore be memorised beforehand. This page shows the right path for Black to take in two very tricky lines.

THE PREVIOUS MOVES WERE:

	Minev	**Kratkovsky**
	(Bulgarian Championship, 1956)	
	White	**Black**
1	P–K4	P–Q3
2	P–Q4	N–KB3
3	N–QB3	P–KN3
4	B–KN5	P–KR3!

Best to make White decide right now where the Bishop is to go. Botvinnik in particular has done well with this move.

The alternative 5 B–K3 is discussed elsewhere in this chapter, and 5 BxN would be quite harmless.

5	B–R4	
5	...	B–N2
6	P–B4	
6	...	P–B4!
7	P–K5?	

See facing page for White's best line.

PLAY NOW CONTINUED:

7	...	N–R4!
8	N–Q5!?	
8	...	PxQP!
9	B–N5 ch	
9	...	B–Q2
10	BxP	Q–R4 ch
11	P–N4	QxB!!

White thinks the game is over.

To shield the Knight from the threatened ... Q–R4 ch.

and Black gets three pieces for the Queen after 12 N–B7 ch KxB, 13 NxQ BxN.

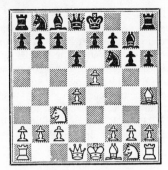

Position after 6 P–K5?

The immediate 6 P–K5? is no better for White, as the following line shows . . .

PLAY NOW CONTINUES:

6 . . .	PxP	
7 PxP	N–N5!	
8 QxQ ch	KxQ	
9 O–O–O ch	B–Q2	
10 P–KB4	P–KN4!	with advantage to Black.

Unzicker–Botvinnik (Moscow, 1956) went quite well for White after: 6 B–K2 P–B4, 7 P–K5 N–R4!, 8 QPxP! N–B5, 9 B–N3 PxKP, 10 QxQ ch KxQ, 11 O–O–O ch B–Q2, 12 B–B3, etc.—so maybe 6 . . . O–O is best for Black.

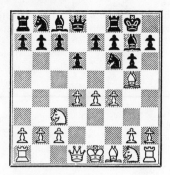

Position after 5 . . . O–O?

THE OPENING MOVES WERE:

The questionable line 4 . . . B–N2 is fraught with many dangers for Black, especially if a discreet . . . P–KR3 is not tacked onto the system afterwards. Apart from the excellent plan Q–Q2 and O–O–O, White can also make life difficult for the Black King by 5 P–KB4, with the idea of either a quick rush with the KRP, or P–K5, depending on how Black plays at his fifth move.

Nettheim   Hamilton
(Australian Correspondence Championship, 1958)

1	P–K4	P–Q3

There is much to be said for the Kotov/Robatsch method here—i.e. 1 . . . P–KN3, 2 . . . B–N2 and 3 . . . P–Q3, which makes 4 B–KN5 pointless.

2	P–Q4	N–KB3
3	N–QB3	P–KN3
4	B–KN5	B–N2

No absolute refutation of this line exists, but White certainly wins many fine games against it!

5	P–B4	O–O?

PLAY NOW CONTINUED:

6	P–K5!	N–K1
7	N–B3	N–Q2

If any improvement is possible for Black, it will have to be on the seventh move. After the text, White's juggernaut KRP gets into his unstoppable stride.

8	P–KR4!	P–KR3
9	P–R5!!	PxB
10	NxP	N–N3
11	B–Q3	P–KB3
12	RPxP	PxN
13	R–R8 ch!	

If 11 . . . P–KB4 then 12 P–KN4! wins.

and Black cannot avoid mate.

Position after 5 . . . P–B4??

An equally severe treatment awaits the oversharp 5 . . . P–B4??, where Black gives up a piece in the hope of getting at the White King before it can castle into safety. But White must be careful to choose the correct (albeit somewhat bizarre) ninth move.

PLAY NOW CONTINUES:

6 P–K5!	**PxQP**

6 . . . KN–Q2, 7 KPxP BPxP, 8 N–N5 the position is hopeless for Black, and 6 . . . PxKP, 7 PxKP will lead eventually to the establishment of a White Knight on Q5.

7 PxN	**PxP**
8 QxP	**Q–K2 ch**
9 QN–K2!	

leaving room for the Queen.

9 . . .	**N–B3**
10 Q–B3	

and White remains a piece up.

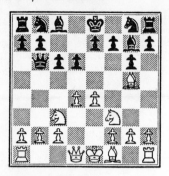

Position after 5 . . . Q–N3?

Even when Black postpones the development of his King's Knight, the move B–KN5 still poses problems. The best way to deal with them is to prod the Bishop with . . . P–KR3, and then (a) leave the Knight at home if the Bishop withdraws along its original diagonal, or (b) go ahead with a straight transposition into the Pirc if the Bishop goes to KR4 instead (where it blocks the possible advance of the White KRP, which can be very nasty). What Black should *not* do is go slavering after the unprotected Poison Pawn at QN7 . . .

THE OPENING MOVES WERE:

	Tal	Tringov
	(Amsterdam, 1964)	
1	P–K4	P–KN3
2	P–Q4	B–N2
3	N–QB3	

White can of course easily transpose into the King's Indian with 3 P–QB4—and in fact such transposition can also be achieved in the Pirc, although I have never yet seen it in a master tournament: **Hartston-Howson,** Cambridgeshire vs Essex, 1968, opened with the moves 1 P–K4 P–Q3, 2 P–QB4 N–KB3, 3 N–QB3 P–KN3, 4 P–Q4 B–N2, etc (and was eventually drawn).

3 . . .	P–Q3
4 N–B3	P–QB3
5 B–KN5	Q–N3?

This move certainly deserves a question mark, since it blocks an eventual advance by the QNP, and thus virtually obliges Black to continue with his highly dangerous meal at QN7. Better is 5 . . . P–KR3!, and if 6 B–K3 then . . . N–Q2 and . . . Q–B2, followed possibly by . . . P–QR3 and . . . P–QN4.

PLAY NOW CONTINUED:

6 Q–Q2!   Quite rightly, Tal feels the sacrifice will be perfectly sound.

6 . . .   **QxNP**   and thus Tringov embarked upon the road to ruin.

The game didn't last much longer: 7 R–QN1 Q–R6, 8 B–QB4 Q–R4, 9 O–O P–K3, 10 KR–K1 P–QR3, 11 B–B4 P–K4, 12 PxP PxP, 13 Q–Q6!! QxN, 14 KR–Q1 N–Q2, 15 BxP ch! KxB, 16 N–N5 ch K–K1, 17 Q–K6 ch Resigns—a typical Tal finish!

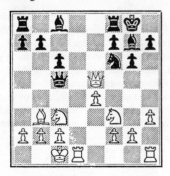

Position after 14 QxKP?

The **Larsen-Penrose** game at Dundee, 1967, was full of interest, both theoretically and tactically. White tried an early B–K3 and Black answered in novel style by pushing his KP and then placing the Queen on K2. Larsen castled Queen's side, as he does so often, but failed to reduce Penrose's counterchances by means of a judicious Knight manoeuvre on the tenth move. Just afterwards White grabbed a "poison pawn" in the centre, with the usual result . . .

THE OPENING MOVES WERE:

Larsen	Penrose
1 N–KB3	P–KN3
2 P–K4	B–N2
3 P–Q4	P–Q3
4 N–QB3	N–KB3
5 B–K3	

A Larsen trademark, but not new—the game **Rossolimo-Reshevsky**, 1963, USA Championship, featured the same line, with Black falling into a little trap on the seventh turn:

5 B–K3 B–N5, 6 B–QB4 P–K3, 7 Q–Q2 N–B3?, 8 N–KN5! P–Q4, 9 B–N5 P–KR3?, 10 NxBP! KxN, 11 P–KR3 regaining the piece with advantage.

5 ...	O–O
6 Q–Q2	P–K4
7 PxP	PxP
8 O–O–O	Q–K2
9 P–KR3	QN–Q2
10 B–QB4?	

10 N–Q5! is much stronger.

10 ...	Q–N5!
11 B–N3	N–QB4

11 ... NxP, 12 NxN QxN would be decidedly unhealthy for Black after 13 KR–K1!

12 BxN	QxQB
13 Q–KN5	P–QB3
14 QxKP?	

Suicidal bravado against such a strong opponent . . . or maybe Larsen simply overlooked Black's 15th move.

PLAY NOW CONTINUED:

14 ... N–Q4!, 15 Q–N5 B–B3, 16 Q–N3 NxN, 17 PxN QxQBP, 18 N–K1 Q–N7 ch, 19 K–Q2 P–QR4, 20 P–QR4 Q–Q5 ch, 21 N–Q3 QxKP, and Black capitalised on his material plus by winning in 40 moves.

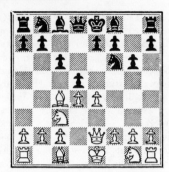

Position after 5 ... P–Q4?

This line needs careful watching by Black. Apart from 5 N–KB3, White can try 5 Q–K2, which also contains a dash of poison. As evidence let me show you a game where I myself was "hooked" by that ultra-sharp player Michael Basman. He found a really beautiful line of play at Southend, 1968, when I tried to push his QB back prematurely as shown here.

THE OPENING MOVES WERE:

Basman	Howson
1 P–K4	P–Q3
2 P–Q4	N–KB3
3 N–QB3	P–KN3
4 B–QB4	P–B3

This alternative to 4 ... B–N2 is quite playable, and is designed to give additional protection to the square Q4 should White eventually get P–K5 in—the Black KN will be able to go to Q4 after ... PxKP.

| 5 Q–K2 | P–Q4? |

But now 5 ... B–N2 is absolutely vital, as the ensuing play clearly demonstrates.

PLAY NOW CONTINUED:

| 6 PxP | PxP |
| 7 B–KN5!! | |

6 ... NxP is no good, because of 7 BxN PxB, 8 Q–K5, etc.

and Black is in a most horrible mess, due to the pin on his KP. The simple 7 ... PxB would leave him with little to hope for after 8 BxN R–N1, 9 O–O–O. So I tried QN–Q2, and lost eventually ... but not because of faulty opening play, surprisingly enough.

The game continued 8 O–O–O!?? (a terrible blunder ... or remarkably inspired play!) PxB, 9 N–N5 B–N2, 10 N–Q6 ch K–B1, 11 NxQBP and Black spent so much time gloating over his extra piece that he eventually succumbed to clock pressure—after refusing the offer of a draw! And so, for once in chess, justice was done.

Position after 5 ... QN–Q2?

Although dangerous, the 4 B–QB4 variation is one of the easiest to deal with if Black plays correctly, because the threat of an eventual ... P–Q4 will force White's Bishop back to QN3 with loss of tempo. In the diagrammed position, however, Black has omitted to castle on the fifth move.

THE OPENING MOVES WERE:

White	Black
1 P–K4	P–Q3
2 P–Q4	N–KB3
3 N–QB3	P–KN3
4 B–QB4	B–N2
5 N–KB3	QN–Q2?

5 ... B–N5? is also bad, because of 6 P–K5 PxP, 7 BxP ch! KxB, 8 NxP ch, etc.

PLAY NOW CONTINUES:

6 P–K5	PxP

There is no salvation to be had in 6 ... N–KN1, 7 BxP ch! KxB, 8 N–KN5 ch and 9 N–K6.

7 PxP	N–R4
8 BxP ch!	KxB
9 N–N5 ch	

and Black has no good move.

Even if Black does play 5 ... O–O, the possibility of P–K5 at a later stage by White must still be guarded against. For example, after 6 O–O the move ... QN–Q2 leads once more to a bad game for Black: 7 P–K5! N–R4, 8 R–K1 N–N3, 9 B–Q3 P–KB4, 10 B–KN5 P–Q4, 11 Q–Q2 with a difficult position for Black.

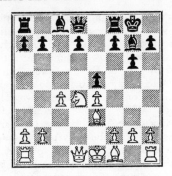

Position after 11 NxN?

One drastic method of holding back the freeing manoeuvre ... P–Q4 is where White plays an early P–QB4, in order to have two pawns trained on the vital square instead of one. The basic disadvantage of this system, which is no doubt the reason for its lack of popularity at the moment, is that Black can put a Knight straight onto Q5 and then back it up with ... P–K4 (as suggested by Bronstein). White must allow the intruder to stay put for a while, or lay himself open to the kind of blistering attack shown below.

THE OPENING MOVES WERE:

	White	Black
1	P–K4	P–QB4
2	N–KB3	N–QB3
3	P–Q4	PxP
4	NxP	P–KN3
5	P–QB4	B–N2
6	B–K3	N–KB3
7	N–B3	

If White tries to prevent Black's next by 7 P–B3, the sharp reply ... Q–N3! has been found to be good for Black in all variations.

7	...	N–KN5!
8	QxN	NxN
9	Q–Q1!	P–K4
10	N–N5!?	

This move is sound enough in itself, but only if the Black Knight is *not* captured at once.

| 10 | ... | O–O |
| 11 | NxN? | |

Correct is 11 Q–Q2, in order to cut out the check on R5 which proves so disastrous after the move played.

PLAY NOW CONTINUES:

11	...	PxN
12	BxP	Q–R4 ch!
13	K–K2	R–K1
14	P–B3	P–Q4!!

and White is virtually lost.

Two possible continuations are: 15 BPxP RxP ch!, 16 PxR B–N5 ch, etc.; and 15 BxB RxP ch, 16 K–B2 Q–B4 ch, 17 K–N3 Q–K6!, threatening ... R–N5 ch (16 K–Q3 is refuted by ... RxP, 17 B–B3 B–B4 ch, etc.).

Position after 6 . . . N–N5??

It's practically a full-time job keeping up with developments in the Sicilian these days. One variation which has had a particularly large amount of attention paid to it is the Dragon system, where Black fianchettoes King's side and takes a chance on the inevitable pawn roller which White throws forward after castling Queen's Rook. The basic trap associated with the early play is shown here, with Black attempting to chase the White QB immediately it goes to K3. This is a very serious error.

THE OPENING MOVES WERE:

White	Black
1 P–K4	P–QB4
2 N–KB3	P–Q3
3 P–Q4	PxP
4 NxP	N–KB3
5 N–QB3	P–KN3
6 B–K3	N–N5??

A terrible blunder which still claims the occasional victim in the lower echelons of club play.

PLAY NOW CONTINUES:

7 B–QN5 ch!

and Black must interpose the Queen's Knight, otherwise his other one will have no protection—i.e. 7 . . . B–Q2, 8 QxN, etc. The forced reply 7 . . . N–QB3 costs him the exchange and a pawn after 8 NxN PxN, 9 BxP ch B–Q2, 10 BxR NxB, 11 PxN QxB.

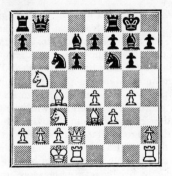

Position after 12 N(4)xP?

PLAY CONTINUES:

12 ...	N–K4!
13 B–K2	BxN
14 NxB	NxBP
15 BxN	QxN

A more sensible line of play is 6 ...
B–N2, 7 P–B3 N–B3, 8 Q–Q2 O–O,
9 B–QB4 B–Q2, 10 O–O–O. Now Black
has a number of interesting continuations
available to him, one of the sharpest
being 10 ... Q–N1!? The basic object
of this peculiar manoeuvre is immediately revealed if White goes straight on
with the King's side advance, as in
Matts-Gufeld, 1967: 11 P–KN4
P–QN4! Now, if either Knight takes the
pawn ...

with a promising attack, since 16 P–K5?
can be answered by QR–N1 threatening
mate.

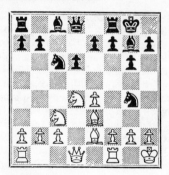

Position after 9 ... N–KN5??

Page 158 shows how ... N–KN5 can prove to be a costly error if White is able to reply with a check on QN5. This page illustrates that the move can also be suspect even after Black has castled. The game in question was played at Bognor in 1969. White shifted his King to R1 on the ninth move, doubtless with the intention of avoiding an awkward check on the diagonal at a later stage should he continue with 10 P–KB4, and Black selected a reply which would have been perfectly alright against the more usual White move 9 Q–Q2.

THE OPENING MOVES WERE:

	I. B. N. Smith	**D. J. P. Gray**
1	P–K4	P–QB4
2	N–KB3	P–Q3
3	P–Q4	PxP
4	NxP	N–KB3
5	N–QB3	P–KN3
6	B–K2	B–N2
7	B–K3	N–QB3
8	O–O	O–O
9	K–R1	

This move suffers from the drawback that Black can liquidate the centre at once, gaining easy equality, by: 9 ... P–Q4!, 10 PxP NxP, 11 QNxN NxN, 12 BxN QxN =.

9 ...	N–KN5??

PLAY NOW CONTINUED:

10	BxN	BxB
11	NxN!	

This sort of interposition (or Zwischenzug, as the Germans call it) also works in the similar variation where White has played 9 P–KB4 instead of 9 K–R1—e.g. 9 ... N–KN5?, 10 BxN BxB, 11 NxN! (although in this case Black can at least creep out with only an inferior position by playing instead 10 ... BxN, 11 BxKB BxB, 12 Q–Q2! (threatening 13 P–B5) ±.

11 ...	BxQ
12 NxQ	BxP
13 NxP	

and White has won a piece.

The next few moves were not without interest, however, since White had to be careful not to lose too many pawns for the piece: 13 ... KR–QN1, 14 QR–QB1 B–Q6, 15 KR–Q1 B–QR3, 16 N–R5 RxP, 17 N–Q5! RxRP, 18 N–B7 R–QB1, 19 NxB RxR, 20 RxR RxN, 21 R–B8 ch B–B1, 22 P–KN3 K–N2, 23 N–B7! and Black had no satisfactory defence against the threatened check on K8.

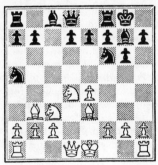

Position after 8 . . . N–QR4?

Even when King's side fianchetto and castling has been completed, the possibility of a Bishop sacrifice on KB2 must never be overlooked. Although both King and Rook guard the pawn, variations do exist where Black cannot conveniently recapture with either. Samuel Reshevsky once found himself in such a dilemma, when paired against the young prodigy Bobby Fischer in the 1959 USA Championship.

THE OPENING MOVES WERE:

	Fischer	Reshevsky
1	P–K4	P–QB4
2	N–KB3	N–QB3
3	P–Q4	PxP
4	NxP	P–KN3
5	N–QB3	B–N2
6	B–K3	N–KB3
7	B–QB4	O–O
8	B–N3	N–QR4?

This move, together with the ninth, loses a pawn for nothing (if Black plays cautiously), or Queen for two minor pieces (if he plays bravely, as Reshevsky did here).

PLAY NOW CONTINUED:

9 P–K5!	N–K1?	

Far better to restrict the loss to two pieces for Rook and two pawns (*and a lousy position!*) by 9 . . . NxB, 10 KPxN NxR, 11 PxB NxP ch, etc—but perhaps he didn't *see* White's next!

10 BxP ch!!	KxB	
11 N–K6!	PxN	

11 . . . KxN leads to mate after 12 Q–Q5 ch K–B4, 13 P–KN4 ch KxP, 14 R–N1 ch K–R5, 15 Q–N2, etc.

12 QxQ

and White won after a protracted struggle.

Reshevsky himself showed how Black can deal with this dangerous variation, when he played **Larry Evans** three years later in the 1962 USA Championship: 8 . . . Q–R4!, 9 P–B3 P–N3, 10 Q–Q2 B–QR3, 11 O–O–O N–K4, 12 K–N1 N–B5 with an equal game.

Position after 8 P–B3?

White's eighth move (B–N3) in the "Fischer" variation is not just a good waiting manoeuvre, but also a sound defensive measure against the possibility of an early . . . Q–N3 counterattack by Black. Fischer himself made the error of omitting the additional move at Portoroz, in 1958, when making his interzonal debut. On this occasion he was lucky in that his opponent, Panno, failed to take proper advantage of the mistake.

THE OPENING MOVES WERE:

	Fischer	Panno
1	P–K4	P–QB4
2	N–KB3	N–QB3
3	P–Q4	PxP
4	NxP	P–KN3

The Accelerated variation, which allows White the option of playing the Maroczy Bind by 5 P–QB4.

5	N–QB3	B–N2
6	B–K3	N–B3
7	B–QB4	O–O
8	P–B3?	

PLAY NOW CONTINUED:

8	. . .	Q–N3!
9	B–N3	

and now Black should have played 9 . . . N–KN5!, 10 PxN BxN, ruining Black's pawn structure irrevocably. Instead, he greedily snapped up the KP with 9 . . . NxP?, and after 10 N–Q5 Q–R4 ch, 11 P–B3 N–B4, 12 NxN QPxN, 13 NxP ch K–R1, 14 NxB QRxN, 15 O–O Fischer had equalised.

Position after 8 P–B3?

The **Fischer-Olafsson** game, at Bled, in 1961, went: 7 ... Q–R4, 8 O–O O–O, 9 N–N3 Q–B2, with no advantage for either side. Here again 8 P–B3? is a serious error, which was in fact perpetrated by **Durao** in his game against **Pustina** at Leipzig, 1960.

PLAY NOW CONTINUED:

8 ...	Q–N5
9 B–N3	NxP!
10 N(4)xN	BxN ch
11 PxB	QxP ch
12 K–K2	Q PxN

with a won game.

Position after 9 Q–Q2?

Where Black plays the quiet ... P–Q3 against 7 B–QB4, the move 8 P–KB3 is perfectly OK, and serves very well to cut out a possible ... N–KN5. But Black can reply with the sharp move 8 ... Q–N3, setting up the triple-pronged threats of ... QxP, ... N–KN5 and ... NxKP. The trap on this page is devoted to a brief examination of these fairly obvious possibilities, say after the typical error Q–Q2.

THE OPENING MOVES WERE:

White	Black
1 P–K4	P–QB4
2 N–KB3	N–QB3
3 P–Q4	PxP
4 NxP	P–KN3
5 N–QB3	B–N2
6 B–K3	N–KB3
7 B–QB4	

7 P–KB3 at once isn't much good, owing to the reply ... O–O, 8 Q–Q2 P–Q4! (or 8 B–QB4 Q–N3!).

7 ...	P–Q3
8 P–KB3	Q–N3
9 Q–Q2?	

White wants to protect the QB, so as to threaten N–B5. The reply 9 Q–Q3? is no better, since it merely helps Black to complete his development after ... N–K4, 10 B–N5 ch B–Q2, 11 Q–K2 Q–B2, etc.

PLAY NOW CONTINUES:

9 ...	NxKP!

Yet another example of the temporary sacrifice of the KN, this time winning a vital pawn now that White's N on Q4 is three times hit and only twice guarded.

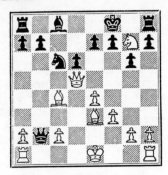

Position after 12 QxN?

PLAY NOW CONTINUES:

12 ...	QxR ch
13 K–B2	

There is of course the tempting reply 9 N–B5!? at White's disposal (best of all, by the way, is probably the simple 9 B–QN5!), which forces 9 ... QxP. Now, after grabbing the piece with 10 NxB ch K–B1, even the strongest player might fall for the lure of 11 N–Q5! NxN, 12 QxN?, since it threatens mate in a position where White is already a piece up. But it loses (12 BxN is correct).

as expected.

After 13 K–K2? Black would eventually win the KB with check—i.e. 13...QxN, 14 B–KR6 B–K3, 15 BxQ ch KxB, 16 Q–Q3 N–K4, etc.

13 ...	Q–B3!

and White has nothing better than 14 B–KR6 K–N1, 15 N–K8 Q–Q5 ch, and Black finishes the exchange and a pawn up.

Position after 13 ... NxRP?

THE OPENING MOVES WERE:

However Black plays in the Dragon, White can always get his RP up to the fifth rank if he wishes, so players using this system of defence must be familiar with the correct techniques necessary to neutralise the King's side pawn storm. All this is explained in depth in *The Sicilian Dragon*, by R. D. Keene, available from Chessman Publications, Birkenhead, and interested readers should purchase this booklet, which costs only 2/6. Here is one variation, typical of many, where Black's Draconian solution of simply removing the offending RP leads to a quick loss.

	Evans	Zuckerman
	(New York, 1967)	
1	P–K4	P–QB4
2	N–KB3	P–Q3
3	P–Q4	PxP
4	NxP	N–KB3
5	N–QB3	P–KN3
6	P–B3	B–N2
7	B–K3	N–B3
8	Q–Q2	O–O
9	O–O–O	NxN!

The old variation 9 ... P–Q4, involving a pawn sacrifice, is now considered insufficient in the light of recent intensive research.

10	BxN	B–K3!
11	K–N1	Q–B2
12	P–KR4	KR–B1
13	P–R5	NxRP?

Correct is 13 ... Q–R4, 14 PxP RPxP, 15 P–R3 QR–N1, with equality.

PLAY NOW CONTINUED:

14	BxB	KxB
15	P–KN4	N–B3
16	Q–R6 ch	K–N1
17	P–K5!	PxP
18	P–N5	N–R4
19	B–Q3	

and Black has no defence to the threat of RxN.

Position after 11 B–B3?

THE OPENING MOVES WERE:

White can of course try to "kill the Dragon" by other means than the P–KB3, B–K3 and O–O–O method. An early P–KB4 is one way, leading often to play similar in many respects to the Austrian Attack against the Pirc. The diagrammed position occurred during the game Basman-Whiteley, Southend, 1968. Black has established his Queen's Knight on QN5, just as in Fischer-Korchnoi (see chapter on Pirc Defence), and is able to gain the advantage with a line closely related to that adopted by Korchnoi.

	Basman	Whiteley
1	P–K4	P–QB4
2	N–KB3	P–Q3
3	P–Q4	PxP
4	NxP	N–KB3
5	N–QB3	P–KN3
6	B–K2	B–N2
7	B–K3	N–QB3
8	P–KB4	O–O
9	N–N3	

In the Pirc, the Knight reaches this square via Q2, and Black's reply is just the same—a quick strike by the QRP.

9	...	P–QR4!
10	P–QR4	N–QN5
11	B–B3?	

White should instead castle at once, leaving Black with a slight initiative.

PLAY NOW CONTINUED:

| 11 | ... | B–KN5! |
| 12 | O–O | |

Attempting to remedy his error, but now Black's other Knight leaps boldly into the fray. The obvious 12 BxB fails against 12 ... NxB, 13 QxN NxP ch, 14 K–B2 NxB, 15 KxN (or 15 Q–K2 N–N5 ch, 16 QxN Q–N3 ch) Q–N3 ch, etc.

12	...	BxB
13	RxB	N–KN5
14	K–R1	NxB

Electing to keep up the positional pressure rather than ruin White's Queen's side with 14 ... BxN.

| 15 | RxN | R–QB1 |
| 16 | Q–K2 | Q–N3 |

and Black's tremendous positional advantage won the game for him on the 26th move.

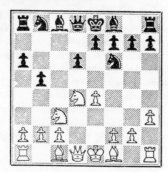

Position after 6 ... P–QN4?

THE OPENING MOVES WERE:

Black's fifth move ... P–QR3, in the Najdorf system, serves two purposes—it prepares for ... P–K4 by cutting out the Bishop check which might otherwise prove awkward, and is also a useful waiting move which forces White to commit himself before Black has done so. The interesting reply 6 P–KR3 (originally suggested by Weaver Adams) has been adopted on numerous occasions by Fischer, one notable instance being his game against Najdorf himself at Varna, 1962. Najdorf's reply, 6 ... P–QN4, has ever since been given a question mark in the tetxbooks, and deservedly so.

	Fischer	Najdorf
1	P–K4	P–QB4
2	N–KB3	P–Q3
3	P–Q4	PxP
4	NxP	N–KB3
5	N–QB3	P–QR3
6	P–KR3	

The best reply now seems to be ... P–K3, preparing to answer a possible P–KN4 with ... P–Q4!, etc. Other tries by Black have turned out badly— at least, they have against Fischer! Here are two continuations:

Fischer-Bolbochan, Stockholm, 1962: 6 ... N–B3, 7 P–KN4 NxN, 8 QxN P–K4, 9 Q–Q3 B–K2, 10 P–N5 N–Q2, 11 B–K3 N–B4, 12 Q–Q2 $\pm$.
Fischer-Reshevsky, USA Championship, 1963: 6 ... P–KN3, 7 P–KN4 B–N2, 8 P–N5 N–R4, 9 B–K2 P–K4, 10 N–N3 N–B5, 11 N–Q5 NxN, 12 QxN $\pm$.

6 ...	P–QN4?

PLAY NOW CONTINUED:

7	N–Q5!	B–N2
8	NxN ch	NPxN
9	P–QB4!	PxP
10	BxP	BxP

7 ... NxP? is refuted by 8 Q–B3!.

Black decides to accept the pawn, rather than struggle on without compensation in a basically inferior position.

11	O–O	P–Q4
12	R–K1!	P–K4
13	Q–R4 ch	N–Q2
14	RxB!!	PxR
15	N–B5	

and Black has no good moves left (he resigned on the 24th turn).

Position after 9 . . . P–K3?

A king's side fianchetto by White on the sixth turn is quite innocuous against good play by Black (characterised normally by . . . P–K4, blocking the diagonal of White's KB). However, if Black tries to refute the sixth move out of hand, either by means of a counter fianchetto on the Queen's side, or by hitting at the apparent weakness on White's KB3, then White retains a strong initiative at the very least.

THE OPENING MOVES WERE:

	White	Black
1	P–K4	P–QB4
2	N–KB3	P–Q3
3	P–Q4	PxP
4	NxP	N–KB3
5	N–QB3	P–QR3
6	P–KN3	P–QN4!?
7	B–N2	B–N2
8	O–O	QN–Q2
9	R–K1	P–K3?

9 . . . R–QN1 seems best.

PLAY NOW CONTINUES:

10 P–K5! BxB, 11 PxN B–N2, 12 PxP BxP, 13 N–B5 and Black can hardly survive much longer.

Position after 10 . . . N(3)xKNP??

The move 6 . . . B–KN5? is very tempting for Black. After all, White appears to be at his weakest with a half-completed fianchetto, and the White Queen will come under fire if White keeps the diagonal open with . . . Q–Q3 (rather than play the obviously questionable . . . P–KB3). But there is more to it: 6 . . . B–N5?, 7 Q–Q3 QN–Q2, 8 P–KR3 N–K4, 9 Q–K3 Q–N3!?, 10 PxB! Now Black realises that 10 . . . QxN, 11 QxQ N–B6 ch, 12 K–Q1 NxQ, 13 B–R3! is not so promising after all, so he tries a Zwischenzug . . .

PLAY NOW CONTINUES:

11	Q–K2	QxN
12	P–B4!	

and a piece is lost.

Position after 14 ... NxP??

When White brings his KB to QB4, and has the KP guarded by the QN, an opportunity often arises for Black to play ... NxKP, NxN P–Q4, forking the two pieces and regaining the sacrificed material with much more freedom in the centre. But he must always beware of the dreaded Zwischenzug appearing before the piece is recaptured. Tal himself fell victim to this kind of trap in his game with Ciric at Wijk aan Zee, 1968.

THE OPENING MOVES WERE:

	Ciric	Tal
1	P–K4	P–QB4
2	N–KB3	N–QB3
3	P–Q4	PxP
4	NxP	N–KB3
5	N–QB3	P–Q3
6	B–QB4	B–Q2
7	P–KR3	NxN
8	QxN	P–KN3
9	O–O	B–N2
10	B–K3	O–O
11	Q–Q3	

Now that Black's QN is gone, this square is a very good one for the White Queen—in marked contrast to Hennings' 11 Q–Q3? on the facing page.

11	...	Q–QR4
12	B–Q4	B–B3
13	P–QR3	

Quite possibly foreseeing Tal's faulty idea, and preparing a crafty refutation.

13	...	P–K4
14	B–K3	NxP??

PLAY NOW CONTINUED:

15	P–QN4	Q–Q1
16	NxN	P–Q4
17	P–N5!	

and Tal suddenly finds himself minus a piece for keeps! The next few moves were 17 ... PxB, 18 QxQ KRxQ, 19 PxB PxP, 20 N–Q2 P–B6, 21 N–B4 and Black conceded the inevitable defeat 20 moves later.

Position after 11 Q–Q3?

PLAY NOW CONTINUED:

Havana, 1967, witnessed a smart piece of work by **Taimanov** as Black against **Hennings** in the same variation. The first six moves were the same as before, and then White played the llne 7 O–O P–KN3, 8 P–KR3 B–N2, 9 B–K3. But then, after 9 ... O–O, 10 B–N3 R–QB1, Hennings decided to put his Queen on Q3 rather than the safer square K2.

11 ...	N–K4
12 Q–K2	RxN!!
13 PxR	NxP
14 Q–K1	Q–B2
15 P–KB3	N–KB3
16 N–K2	P–QR3
17 R–Q1	N–B5

Not ... NxQBP?? because of 16 P–KB4! winning a piece.

and White was finally squashed to death on the 35th move.

Position after 6 ... B–N2?

If White plays P–B4 on the sixth move, rather than B–K2 or B–K3, Black cannot proceed blithely with his fianchetto, as is demonstrated below. He must instead try ... QN–Q2 or ... N–QB3, both of which need careful handling. If 6 ... B–N2? is played, White can achieve a definite advantage by 7 P–K5 however Black continues, although one variation (7 ... N–KR4) is not quite so easy as it looks, as is discussed on the facing page.

THE OPENING MOVES WERE:

	White	Black
1	P–K4	P–QB4
2	N–KB3	P–Q3
3	P–Q4	PxP
4	NxP	N–KB3
5	N–QB3	P–KN3
6	P–B4	
6 ...		B–N2?

The Levenfish Variation.

PLAY NOW CONTINUES:

| 7 | P–K5! | PxP |

This seems best, although 7 ... N–KR4 can also be tried, and 7 ... B–N5 is just about playable. In the latter case, White must remember to check with the KB on QN5 before moving his Queen up to Q3, thus forcing Black to disrupt his position while dealing with the check.

| 8 | PxP | KN–Q2 |

Otherwise the check on QN5 will once again prove very awkward for Black.

| 9 | P–K6! | |

and Black's position is in ruins after say 9 ... PxP, 10 NxP BxN ch, 11 PxB Q–N3, 12 B–QB4, etc.

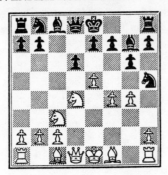

Position after 8 P–KN4?

If Black tries 7 . . . N–KR4!? instead, White must on no account "trap" the Knight with 8 P–KN4?

PLAY NOW CONTINUES:

| 8 . . . | NxP!! |
| 9 BxN | PxP |

and White is tangled in his own web.

Once again we find that the magic check on QN5 is the best continuation. For example, 8 B–N5 ch B–Q2, 9 P–K6! PxP, 10 NxP BxN ch, 11 PxB Q–R4, 12 B–Q2! with a tremendous position.

Position after 7 P–KN3?

The actual moment of starting a fianchetto, when only the NP has moved is the most vulnerable particularly when enemy pieces are already developed. Very often a fianchetto under these circumstances constitutes an attempt to hold on to an extra pawn, as is the case here.

THE OPENING MOVES WERE:

	White	Black
1	P–Q4	N–KB3
2	P–QB4	P–K4
3	PxP	N–K5!?

The Fajarowicz System, leading to play full of traps for both sides.

4	P–QR3	P–Q3
5	N–KB3	N–QB3
6	PxP	

6 Q–B2 is the best move here. The reply 6 . . . B–B4 is not to be feared, as was shown in the game **Reshevsky-Bisguier**, 1954, which continued: 7 N–B3! NxBP, 8 QxB NxR, 9 P–K6 PxP, 10 QxP ch Q–K2, 11 Q–Q5 P–KR3, 12 P–KN3 with a winning advantage.

6	. . .	BxP
7	P–KN3?	

7 P–K3 or 7 QN–Q2 would allow White to struggle wearily on, although his position is now terribly passive.

PLAY NOW CONTINUES:

7	. . .	NxBP!
8	Q–B2	

8 KxN? loses the Queen after 8 . . . BxP ch!

8	. . .	NxR
9	B–N2	NxP
10	PxN	BxP ch

and Black is miles ahead on material.

BIRD'S OPENING

Position after 8 N–K5?

THE OPENING MOVES WERE:

	White	Black
1	P–KB4	P–Q4
2	N–KB3	N–KB3
3	P–K3	P–KN3
4	P–QB4!	

4	...	B–N2
5	N–QB3	O–O
6	Q–N3!?	

6	...	PxP
7	BxP	N–QB3
8	N–K5?	

PLAY NOW CONTINUES:

8	...	NxN
9	PxN	N–Q2!
10	BxP ch	K–R1!

Until quite recently, 1 P–KB4 was considered a rather passive way to start the game, since in most lines Black is able to take an iron grip on the centre. However, Larsen in particular has shown that the advance of a flank pawn on the King's side can be effectively combined with a similar push on the other wing. The diagrammed position arises from just such a manoeuvre (4 P–QB4), followed by a sharp but questionable attack on the Black KBP.

Without doubt the best sort of continuation here. **Larsen-Spassky**, Amsterdam, 1964, involved a similar Queen's side advance:
4 P–QN4! B–N2, 5 B–N2 O–O, 6 B–K2 B–N5, 7 O–O P–B3, 8 P–QR4 QN–Q2, 9 N–R3 with equality.

Too optimistic. Capablanca analysed this position extensively, and proved beyond reasonable doubt that 6 P–Q4 is best at this stage.

and White is virtually lost. For example, 11 P–K6 N–QB4, 12 Q–B4 BxP!,! 13 BxB N–Q6 ch, 14 K–K2 R–B7 ch, 15 K–Q1 NxP ch! and wins.

Position after 11 P–Q4

Nor can White escape retribution by means of a belated 11 P–Q4, because a second pawn sacrifice—which has to be accepted—leaves Black with an "embarrassment of riches" in the shape of *two* promising piece offers.

PLAY NOW CONTINUES:

11 . . .	P–K3!
12 BxP	NxP!!

or 12 . . . BxP, both of which sacrifices give Black a tremendous attack if accepted.

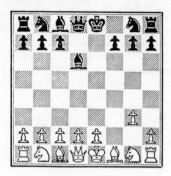

Position after 4 P–KN3??

Now that Larsen has popularised the ancient Bird's Opening once again, the violent From Gambit will no doubt be seen in master practice from time to time, although I have been unable to unearth any good games which have not transposed straight away into a King's Gambit by 2 P–K4. Those bold players of the White pieces who decide to accept the From—and there is no theoretical reason why they should not—must avoid an early King's-side fianchetto like the plague, since it will always lead to serious difficulties.

THE OPENING MOVES WERE:

White	Black
1 P–KB4	P–K4!?
2 PxP	P–Q3
3 PxP	

Failure to accept the gambit at this stage will give Black an excellent position after 3 N–KB3 PxP, 4 P–K4 B–QB4, etc.

3 ...	BxP
4 P–KN3??	

Now that he has the pawn in his pocket, White must play energetically to reduce Black's counterchances to a minimum. One of the best lines at White's disposal is 4 N–KB3 P–KN4!, 5 P–Q4 P–N5, 6 N–K5! BxN, 7 PxB QxQ ch, 8 KxQ N–QB3, 9 B–B4—and Black won't find it so easy to get his pawn back.

PLAY NOW CONTINUES:

4 ...	P–KR4!

Yes ... it's as simple as that! No lengthy combination—Black just pushes the RP to the fifth rank, and White can hardly save the game, no matter how he twists and turns.

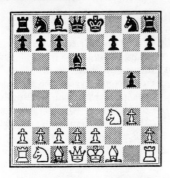

Position after 5 P-KN3?

The attempted fianchetto at the fifth turn is better than the one at the fourth, but still leaves White in a tight spot if Black chooses the right sixth move. The game **Schenk-Spielmann,** Vienna, 1911, has never yet been improved on as far as Black's play is concerned. Schenk tried 4 N-KB3 P-KN4!, 5 P-KN3? . . .

PLAY NOW CONTINUED:

5 . . .	P-N5
6 N-R4	N-K2!

Not 6 . . . B-K2?, because White's QB will then be able to defend the King's side adequately from the KB4 square—e.g. 7 N-N2 P-KR4, 8 P-Q4 P-R5, 9 B-KB4 etc.

7 P-Q4	N-N3
8 N-N2	N-QB3
9 P-K3	P-KR4
10 B-Q3	P-R5

Threatening . . . NxP!

with a crushing attack. The game might well continue 11 BxN PxB, 12 PxP RxP!, etc.

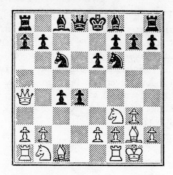

Position after 7 ... PxP?

If White chooses the quiet N–KB3 at the fifth turn, and Black replies ... P–QB4, the position bears a resemblance to the Darga-Pachman Grunfeld variation mentioned on page 62. The similarity becomes even more marked in the event of the logical continuation 6 O–O N–QB3, 7 Q–R4. Now once again, as in the Grunfeld, the move 7 ... PxP? is questionable.

THE OPENING MOVES WERE:

	White	Black
1	P–Q4	N–KB3
2	P–QB4	P–K3
3	P–KN3	P–Q4
4	B–N2	PxP
5	N–KB3	P–QB4
6	O–O	N–QB3
7	Q–R4	
7	...	PxP?

See facing page for the trappy 7 N–K5.

PLAY NOW CONTINUES:

8	NxP!	QxN
9	BxN ch	B–Q2
10	R–Q1!	BxB
11	QxB ch!	PxQ
12	RxQ	

with a clear advantage.

Position after 7 ... NxP??

PLAY WOULD THEN CONTINUE:

8 P–K3!

The alternative 7 N–K5 was **Korchnoi's** choice in his game against **Ivkov** in the 1964 USSR vs Yugoslavia match, at Leningrad. That particular encounter continued 7 ... B–Q2!, 8 NxN BxN, 9 BxB ch PxB, 10 Q–R4 Q–N3, 11 PxP BxP, 12 QxBP O–O, 13 N–Q2 with a minimal plus for White. But what if Black decides to pluck that luscious fruit on Q5?

and Black loses the exchange however he retreats the Knight, due to the threat to his KBP if the Queens go off, or to his QR in the event of ... N–QB3, 9 NxN.

Position after 14 N–K1??

A King's fianchetto by White combined with the moves B–KN5 and KR–Q1 leaves a slight weakness at KB2, which has to be watched very carefully if Black chooses counterplay involving ... P–QB4, QPxP BxP. Larsen fell for a very simple trap embodying this theme at Havana, 1966, in his game with Portisch. Possibly it was the unusual nature of the danger that caused him to make the blunder N–K1??

THE OPENING MOVES WERE:

	Larsen	Portisch
1	P–Q4	P–Q4
2	P–QB4	P–K3
3	N–KB3	B–K2
4	P–KN3	N–KB3
5	B–N2	O–O
6	O–O	PxP

See facing page for a trap arising from ... PxP on the fourth move.

7	Q–B2	P–QR3
8	QxBP	

8 P–QR4 might have been better here, since now Black is able to expand his Queen's side without difficulty.

8	...	P–QN4
9	Q–N3	B–N2
10	KR–Q1	QN–Q2
11	B–KN5	P–QB4
12	PxP	Q–B2
13	QN–Q2	BxP

No danger in this position. But Larsen's next move takes the guard off his KB, with fatal results.

14 N–K1??

PLAY NOW CONTINUED:

14	...	BxP ch!
15	KxB	Q–B4 ch
16	P–K3	N–N5 ch
17	K–N1	BxB
18	NxB	QxB

and, a pawn down with a ruined position, Larsen lasted only another half-dozen moves.

Position after 10 QxQP??

PLAY NOW CONTINUES:

   10 ...   **P–K4!**

When Black plays 4 ... PxP (after say the moves 1 P–Q4 N–KB3, 2 P–QB4 P–K3, 3 P–KN3 P–Q4, 4 B–N2), White can check on QR4 and take the pawn back at once. Alternatively, he may decide to continue with 6 QN–Q2 if Black parries the check with ... QN–Q2. In the latter case, White must avoid the temptation to try for too much. For example, in the following variation— 6 ... P–QB4!, 7 NxP PxP, 8 B–KB4 B–K2, 9 N–Q6 ch K–B1!, it is most unwise to be greedy with 10 QxQP??

and a piece is lost!

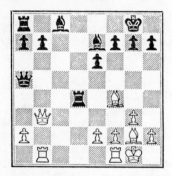

Position after 14 ... RxP?

THE OPENING MOVES WERE:

In recent master practice it has been found advantageous for White to delay P–Q4 slightly, in order to avoid early counter-thrusts by Black designed to gain quick equality through pawn exchanges in the centre. When this happens Black will often play ... P–Q4 himself in an attempt to precipitate the desired exchanges. But in this case Black must always beware of the special problems posed down on the first and second ranks of his QR and QN files, due to the presence of both White Bishops poised in threatening positions on White's King's side, as shown in the diagram.

	Smyslov	Tolush
	(Moscow, 1961)	
1	P–QB4	N–KB3
2	N–KB3	P–K3
3	N–B3	P–QB4
4	P–KN3	P–Q4

Boldly occupying the centre, much as Tarrasch might have done half a century before.

5	PxP	NxP
6	B–N2	N–B3
7	O–O	B–K2
8	P–Q4	NxN!?

Playable enough, I suppose, but 8 ... PxP is probably best of all.

9	PxN	O–O
10	R–N1	Q–R4
11	Q–N3	R–Q1
12	B–B4!	

Black's set-up is now very similar to various lines in the Grunfeld Defence, but with the White pieces much more actively placed. Tolush now sees White's temporary offer of a pawn at Q4 as a possible peace overture, since the resulting mass slaughter on the Queen's side seems to lead to absolute equality. But there is more to it . . .

12	...	PxP
13	NxP	NxN
14	PxN	RxP?

PLAY NOW CONTINUED:

15	BxP	BxB
16	QxB	Q–Q1
17	B–N8!	

trying to guard against B–K3 winning the exchange, and the game.

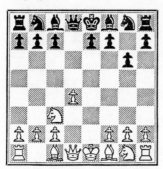

Position after 4 ... P-KN3?

THE OPENING MOVES WERE:

Fischer	Robatsch
1 P-K4	P-Q4
2 PxP	QxP
3 N-QB3	Q-Q1
4 P-Q4	P-KN3?

PLAY NOW CONTINUED:

5 B-KB4	B-N2
6 Q-Q2!	
6 ...	N-KB3
7 O-O-O	P-B3
8 B-KR6	
8 ...	O-O
9 P-KR4	Q-R4
10 P-R5!	PxP
11 B-Q3	QN-Q2
12 KN-K2	R-Q1
13 P-KN4!	

The "Achilles heel" of the fianchetto position is undoubtedly the square R3, which normally has only the Bishop to guard it. If the opponent can force his way into this point with a Bishop, backed up usually by the Queen, then the only good defence is B-R1, leaving the position blocked, and the square N2 still protected by the fianchetto Bishop. However, if the defending Rook is still on B1, then this manoeuvre is obviously not possible. The diagrammed position occurred during the game between Fischer and Robatsch at Varna, 1962, with Black about to embark on a completely inappropriate fianchetto.

The move 2 ... N-KB3 is a good alternative.

"Central" play, starting with ... N-KB3, is much superior here. Now White goes straight for the Achilles heel.

A move Robatsch must have overlooked.

What else can he do? 6 ... BxP?, 7 O-O-O P-QB4, 8 N-N5 loses at once; and 6 ... QxP, 7 QxQ BxQ, 8 N-N5 B-N3, 9 BxP is not much better.

The trap is sprung, and White will now penetrate the King's position at will. It is well worth memorising the next few moves, as being typical of immaculate play against an incorrect fianchetto.

10 ... NxP would be easily refuted by 11 B-K2 N-KB3, 12 BxB KxB, 13 Q-R6 ch K-N1, 14 N-K4 etc.

and there is no defence after White's QR comes to KN1. Robatsch resigned on the 20th move.

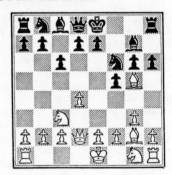

Position after 6 ... P–KR3?

THE OPENING MOVES WERE:

Where Black chooses to counter White's King's fianchetto with one of his own in the Dutch (an idea first popularised by a group of Soviet masters centred upon the city of Leningrad), he must be prepared to answer the sharp 4 N–QB3 with sharp countermoves of his own. Otherwise White's intended P–K4 will be very powerful.

White	Black
1 P–Q4	P–KB4

One disadvantage of the Leningrad System is that Black cannot play the waiting move 1 ... P–K3, but must immediately advance the KBP and take a chance on the outcome of a possible Staunton Gambit (2 P–K4!?).

| 2 P–KN3 | |

By playing the opening this way round, White cuts out any counterplay which Black might conjure up against 2 P–QB4, and also retains the option of 4 N–QB3 against a possible Leningrad.

2 ...	N–KB3
3 B–N2	P–KN3
4 N–QB3	

4 N–KB3 is a solid alternative.

| 4 ... | B–N2 |
| 5 B–KN5 | P–QB3 |

See facing page for a discussion of the more active 5 ... N–QB3?!

| 6 Q–Q2 | P–KR3? |

6 ... O–O is essential here.

PLAY NOW CONTINUES:

| 7 BxN | BxB |
| 8 P–K4! | |

and Black must weaken his King's position irretrievably, in order to eliminate the menacing White KP. The only reasonable line seems to be 8 ... PxP, 9 BxP K–B2, whereupon White continues with 10 O–O–O! etc. ±.

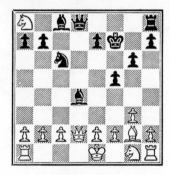

Position after 10 NxR??

The aggressive 5 ... N–QB3?! is better than it looks, and is designed to put another piece "on" White's QP so that he cannot play P–K4 with absolute impunity. One very fine example of good play for both sides is **Botvinnik-Kopilov,** USSR, 1951, which continued: 6 Q–Q2 P–Q4!, 7 BxN BxB, 8 NxP BxP, 9 NxP ch! Now Kopilov found the clever 9 ... K–B2! (9 ... QxB? leaves White with the initiative after 10 BxN ch and 11 QxB). White must on no account take the Rook, because ...

PLAY WOULD THEN CONTINUE:

10 ...	BxP ch!
11 K–Q1	QxQ ch
12 KxQ	R–Q1 ch
13 K–B3	B–Q5 ch

and the White King will have to cope with the hostile attentions of four Black pieces, virtually without assistance from his badly placed entourage.

Botvinnik actually played 10 N–KB3, and an equal position resulted after 10 ... BxP ch!, 11 KxB QxN.

DUTCH DEFENCE

Position after 11 ... QxR?

THE OPENING MOVES WERE

The King's side fianchetto has been found to be an excellent way of countering the Dutch Defence. White develops in a straightforward manner, and then forces P–K4 as quickly as possible. The basic trap in the position, after exchanges have taken place on K4, is shown here, the White Rook being captured by the Black Queen.

	White	Black
1	P–Q4	P–KB4
2	P–KN3	P–K3
3	B–N2	N–KB3
4	N–KB3	B–K2
5	O–O	O–O
6	P–B4	P–Q3

If Black nips on to K5 while it is still unprotected, with 6 ... N–K5, White can reply 7 P–Q5! with an excellent game in the centre.

7	N–B3	Q–K1
8	R–K1	Q–N3
9	P–K4	NxP
10	NxN	PxN
11	RxP	QxR?

PLAY NOW CONTINUES:

    12 N–R4!   and Black loses his Queen.

If Black avoids that pitfall, and plays instead the recommended move 11 ... N–B3!, White in turn must exercise great care if he wishes to retain the initiative. For example, if he fails to choose either:

12 Q–K2 B–B3, 13 B–Q2 P–K4, 14 PxP (**Aronson-Tal**, 1957);
or 12 R–K2 P–K4, 13 PxP B–N5, 14 PxP! BxP, 15 Q–Q5 ch K–R1, 16 N–R4 (**Penrose-Hindle**, 1959);
and tries instead 12 R–K1?, then Black soon gets on top, as was demonstrated in the **Neikirch-Larsen** game at Portoroz, 1958:
12 ... N–N5!, 13 P–QR3 N–B7, 14 N–R4 BxN, 15 B–K4 NxKR!, 16 BxQ N–B6 ch, 17 K–N2, PxB, 18 PxB NxP ch, 19 K–N3 N–B4 ch, 20 K–N2 P–N3, 21 B–N5 B–N2 ch, 22 K–B1 P–B4 with strong pressure.

Position after 16 . . . B–QR3?

THE OPENING MOVES WERE:

One of the most interesting games at Nathanya, 1968, was **Fischer–U. Geller,** in which both players skated on thin ice around the possibility of BxQP. Black set a trap to try and lure White into an unsound pseudo-sacrifice on the 15th move, but Fischer saw that the most he could hope for in the line at that stage was somewhat dubious "equality" with KR–QN1, taking the Rook away from the main field of battle. So the critical moment passed . . . and U. Geller then proceeded to walk straight into a *sound* combination on the same lines two moves later!

	Fischer	U. Geller
1	P–K4	P–K3
2	P–Q3	P–Q4
3	N–Q2	P–QB4
4	P–KN3	N–KB3
5	B–N2	B–K2
6	KN–KB3	O–O
7	O–O	N–QB3
8	R–K1	Q–B2
9	P–K5	N–Q2
10	Q–K2	P–QN4
11	P–KR4	P–QR4
12	N–KB1	N–Q5
13	NxN	PxN
14	B–KB4	R–R3!
15	N–R2!	

Fischer realises that an eventual . . . RxKP could be a winner for Black if White tries 15 BxQP? For example, 15 . . . B–QN5!, 16 KR–QB1 (the abject 16 KR–QN1 probably just holds the position) PxB, 17 P–K6 RxP!, 18 QxR QxB!!, 19 QxN QxR etc—or 16 KR–Q1 PxB, 17 P–K6 RxP!, 18 QxR QxB!!, 19 QxN Q–B6!, 20 N–R2 QxR ch, etc.

15 . . .	R–B3	
16	QR–QB1	B–R3?	*Now* the sacrifice works.

PLAY THEN CONTINUED:

17 BxQP! PxB, 18 P–K6 and now . . . RxP would fail because the Knight on Q2 is unprotected after 19 QxR QxB. So Black had to play the humble 18 . . . Q–Q1, whereupon Fischer quickly forced a win by 19 PxN R–K3, 20 Q–N4 P–KB4, 21 Q–R5 QxP, 22 N–KB3 P–KN3, 23 Q–R6 B–B3, 24 RxR QxR, 25 B–K5! BxB, 26 R–K1 P–B5, 27 RxB Q–Q2, 28 P–R5 PxNP, 29 RPxP!! PxP ch, 30 KxP PxP, 31 QxP ch Q–N2, 32 R–N5! etc.

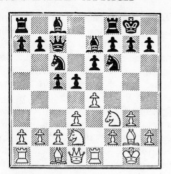

Position after 8 ... Q–B2

This type of line can arise out of either the French Defence, or Sicilian Defence with 2 ... P–K3. If Black places his King's Knight on KB3 rather than K2 then he must take care with his Queen if the game follows the usual channels with P–K5, B–KB4, QN–KB1–K3, and so on by White. The diagrammed position is taken from R. D. Keene's excellent book *Flank Openings*, and illustrates not an outright tactical blunder by Black, but rather a positional error.

THE OPENING MOVES WERE:

Ciocaltea	Kozma
(Sochi, 1962)	
1 N–KB3	P–QB4
2 P–KN3	N–KB3
3 B–N2	P–Q4
4 O–O	N–B3
5 P–Q3	P–K3
6 QN–Q2	B–K2
7 P–K4	O–O
8 R–K1	Q–B2?

Better to strike out immediately with 8 ... P–QN4, leaving the Queen on Q1 for the time being.

PLAY NOW CONTINUED:

9 Q–K2!

No need for White to worry about 9 ... N–Q5, because the Knight can just be taken off. The backward pawn on QB2 will be easy to defend, and Black's doubled QPs will hamstring his own flank attack on the Queen's side while White proceeds unhindered on the opposite wing.

9 ...	P–QN4
10 P–K5	N–Q2
11 N–B1	P–QR4
12 P–KR4	B–R3
13 B–B4	P–N5
14 N–K3!	R–R2
15 P–R5	R–QB1?

Either not realising the danger of a possible sacrifice on Q4, or perhaps under-estimating its power.

16 P–R6	P–N3
17 NxP!	

and Black must either lose a pawn for nothing, or allow White to smash through in the centre after 17 ... PxN, 18 P–K6.

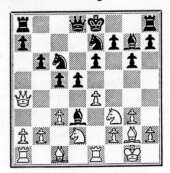

Position after 10 . . . BxQP?

When Black plays . . . KN–K2 instead of . . . N–KB3 against the King's Indian Attack, thus making it more difficult for White to proceed with a clear-cut plan such as R–K1, P–K5, B–KB4, N–KB1, P–KR4 and so forth, the move P–QB3 is often a convenient "pot-boiler" to play while awaiting concrete evidence of Black's intentions. The reply . . . P–QN3 and . . . B–QR3 then becomes a likely proposition to be considered. However, it cannot be ventured without due care, particularly if the White Rook is already on K1 and the Black King remains uncastled.

THE OPENING MOVES WERE:

White	Black
1 P–K4	P–K3
2 P–Q3	P–QB4
3 N–KB3	N–QB3
4 P–KN3	P–KN3

Thus the original French Defence transposes quietly into a King's Indian Attack.

5 B–N2	B–N2
6 O–O	KN–K2
7 P–QB3	P–Q4
8 QN–Q2	P–QN3
9 R–K1	B–QR3?
10 Q–R4!	

9 . . . O–O is better.

Lee–Keene, Southend, 1968, featured the humble retreat 10 . . . B–N2, and White retained a good initiative with 11 PxP PxP, 12 P–Q4 O–O, 13 PxP PxP, 14 Q–R3!, etc.

10 . . .	BxQP??

PLAY NOW CONTINUES:

11 PxP	P–QN4
12 Q–R6	N–QN1
13 Q–N7	

11 . . . PxP allows 12 QxN ch, and 11 . . . QxP fails to 12 N–Q4.

and Black's position caves in **very** quickly.

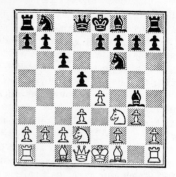

Position after 5 P–KN3??

One of the soundest methods of countering the King's Indian Attack is to quickly bring the QB to KN5, and then set up the pawn phalanx QB3–Q4–K3 to hamper the action of White's fianchettoed Bishop. The system is quite passive in the early stages, but there is one way in which White can go wrong, particularly if he happens to have started with P–K4 on the first move.

THE OPENING MOVES WERE:

	White	Black
1	P–K4	P–QB3
2	P–Q3	

Not finding the Caro-Kann Defence to his taste, White transposes immediately into the KIA.

	White	Black
2	...	P–Q4
3	N–Q2	

Otherwise Black will force the Queens off with ... PxP.

	White	Black
3	...	N–KB3
4	KN–KB3	B–KN5

It hardly seems credible that a serious error could be possible in such an opening, as early as the fifth move. But it's there alright!

	White	Black
5	P–KN3??	

5 P–KR3 is correct, more or less obliging Black to capture the Knight.

PLAY NOW CONTINUES:

	White	Black
5	...	PxP
6	PxP	NxP!

and White will lose a piece if he recaptures—the same theme should be watched for in some variations of the "Pirc with B–KN5".

Position after 6 ... P–K4?

Having seen how Pawn to K4 can be an embarrassment to White in the opening stages of the game, let us now examine a case where the same move in the same opening led swiftly to practically a lost game for Black. The example chosen is **Botvinnik-Szilagyi**, Amsterdam, 1966, which started 1 P–KN3 P–Q4, 2 N–KB3 P–QB3, 3 B–N2 B–KN5, 4 P–Q3 N–Q2, 5 P–KR3 BxN, 6 BxB. Now Szilagyi cut right across the basic strategy of this defensive system with 6 ... P–K4?

PLAY NOW CONTINUED:

7 N–Q2	KN–KB3
8 P–K4	PxP
9 PxP	B–B4
10 O–O	Q–K2
11 P–QB3	O–O
12 P–QN4!	

and suddenly Black's minor pieces find themselves with no good squares to aim for.

In another few moves Black's forces were completely shut in: 12 ... B–N3, 13 P–QR4 KR–Q1, 14 Q–B2 QR–QB1, 15 B–K2 P–QB4, 16 P–N5 N–K1, 17 N–B4 N–Q3, 18 B–KN5! P–B3, 19 B–K3 NxN, 20 BxN ch K–R1, 21 P–R5 B–B2, 22 KR–Q1 N–B1, 23 Q–R2 RxR ch, 24 RxR R–Q1, 25 RxR BxR, 26 P–R6 P–QN3, and White forced his way into the position by reversing the positions of his Q and B on the QR2–KN8 diagonal.

LARSEN/ALEKHINE DEFENCE

Position after 15 ... QxP??

Larsen has a habit of grafting a fianchetto on to even well-known opening variations at the most unlikely moments. This often tends to upset his opponents, even if the graft turns out to be unsuccessful. On this page we find Larsen tinkering with what is normally a stereotyped defence. Both times he gets the worst of it, although managing eventually to salvage half a point from the Yanofsky game. Still, the "mistakes" of today are often the "best play" of tomorrow.

THE OPENING MOVES WERE:

R. Byrne	Larsen
(Monte Carlo, 1968)	
1 P–K4	N–KB3
2 P–K5	N–Q4
3 N–QB3	NxN
4 NPxN	P–QN3!?

This move looks weak, and certainly would have been shown to be weak if Byrne had played 5 Q–B3 N–QB3, 6 P–K6! ruining Black's pawn formation.

5 P–KB4	B–N2
6 N–KB3	P–K3
7 P–Q4	P–Q3
8 B–Q3	B–K2
9 O–O	N–QB3
10 Q–K1	Q–Q2

White's big centre is difficult to handle, no matter what Larsen does.

11 PxP	QxP
12 N–KN5	P–KR3
13 N–K4	Q–Q2
14 P–B5!	O–O–O

A Larsen trademark if ever there was one.

15 PxP	QxP?

An uncharacteristic tactical blunder.

PLAY NOW CONTINUED:

16 Q–KB2!!

and the threat of 17 N–B5 followed by 18 B–B5 is going to cost Larsen material, no matter how he plays. The game continued 16 ... NxP, 17 N–N3 Q–QB3, 18 PxN RxP, 19 N–B5, and Byrne won on the 42nd move.

Position after 10 ... NxP?

PLAY NOW CONTINUED:

11 NxP	Q–Q2
12 N–B5	Q–B3
13 NxB!	

13 ...	PxN
14 BxN!	PxB
15 Q–Q4	

At Winnipeg the previous year, against **Yanofsky, Larsen** had also found himself in hot water after an Alekhine-fianchetto. Here are the opening moves of the game: 1 P–K4 N–KB3, 2 P–K5 N–Q4, 3 P–Q4 P–Q3, 4 N–KB3 PxP, 5 NxP P–KN3, 6 B–QB4 B–K3, 7 N–QB3 B–N2, 8 N–K4. The opening is already beginning to look like nothing on earth—and things get worse for Larsen very quickly as he angles for a chance to play his beloved ... O–O–O, 8 ... BxN!?, 9 PxB N–QB3, 10 N–B5 NxP?

Now 13 Q–Q4, which Larsen may have been expecting, could indeed have been adequately answered by ... O–O–O! But the move Yanofsky chooses instead wrecks Black's position completely.

The alternative 13 ... QxB?? loses to 14 QxN! QxQ, 15 NxP ch.

and Yanofsky is well on top—although he only drew the game eventually.

Position after 7 ... N–QR4??

The Soviet master Sokolsky has played an enormous number of games with this opening, some of them of great beauty. The top diagram shows a position he reached at Munich, 1958. Black has just played 7 ... N–QR4??

THE OPENING MOVES WERE:

	Sokolsky	Strugash
1	P–QN4	P–K4
2	B–N2	P–KB3
3	P–K4	BxP
4	B–QB4	N–QB3?!
5	P–KB4!	PxP?
6	N–KR3!	KN–K2
7	NxP	N–QR4

Inviting White to take his pawn back by 5 BxN RxB, 6 Q–R5 ch K–B1, 7 QxRP. But Sokolsky prefers to keep the pressure up.

5 ... P–Q3 would be more consistent with his previous move.

There is nothing better, since the King's side is already irretrievably weakened.

A desperate attempt to shift the tormenting Bishop. But now Sokolsky clinched victory with a lovely double sacrifice.

PLAY NOW CONTINUED:

8 BxP!! R–KB1 (he dare not take either Bishop, in view of the deadly 9 Q–R5 ch), 9 N–R5! NxB (9 ... RxB fails to 10 NxR ch PxN, 11 Q–R5 ch N–N3, 12 B–N8!, etc), 10 NxP ch K–B2, 11 O–O K–N1, 12 Q–R5 RxN (otherwise 13 Q–N5 will prove unanswerable), 13 RxR N–N3, 14 RxN! PxR, 15 QxP K–R1, 16 N–K8 Q–K2, 17 N–B6 Resigns. Marvellous!

Position after 10 ... B–K2??

PLAY NOW CONTINUED:

11 B–B7 ch!!

The parsimonious 4 ... N–K2 (see also page 198) was featured in **Kata-limov-Ilivitski,** USSR, 1959. White selected the strong reply 5 Q–R5 ch— 5 P–KB4 is also good—and the game continued 5 ... N–N3, 6 P–KB4 PxP, 7 P–QR3! (designed to either force the Bishop back to a bad square, or provoke the loosening ... P–Q4) P–Q4, 8 BxQP P–QB3, 9 B–N3 Q–R4!, 10 P–K5!? (an extraordinary conception which paid handsome dividends out of all proportion to its true worth—since it induced Black to play 10 ... B–K2??

and Ilivitski resigned, since he cannot capture the Bishop without losing his Queen to P–K6 ch, and the KN is in consequence lost for nothing after 12 BxN.

The reply 10 ... B–B4! would have set an amusing counter-trap, since White loses *his* Queen to the same Bishop move which has just caused Black to resign, if he plays 11 PxP??

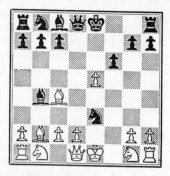

Position after 7 ... N–K6!??

THE OPENING MOVES WERE:

The variation where White offers a permanent sacrifice of the NP for the sake of quick development is full of hidden dangers for Black. Nevertheless, if he defends coolly, White's attack can be halted with a quick countersacrifice ... P–Q4. In the diagrammed position, Black has played this excellent move, but followed it up by first mistakenly recapturing on Q4, and then falling for the lure of a further Knight move which appears to threaten virtually everything under the sun. How can such a glorious move be parried, Black wonders ...

	White	Black
1	P–QN4	P–K4
2	B–N2	P–KB3
3	P–K4	BxP
4	B–B4	N–K2
5	P–KB4!	P–Q4!

If Black grabs the KBP instead, then 6 P–QB3 and 7 P–Q4 give White an overwhelming centre—and Black cannot then strike back with ... P–Q4 because Q–R5 ch, putting an additional piece in line with Q5, will be possible after 8 PxQP.

6	KPxP	NxP!?

6 ... B–Q3! seems strongest here, since the alternative 6 ... PxP allows White to continue with the harmonious development 7 Q–B3 and 8 N–K2.

7	PxP!	

Now Black is in grave difficulties, but might just be able to scramble out with something like 7 ... P–QN4?!, 8 BxP ch P–B3. However, he just cannot resist temptation ...

7	...	N–K6!??

The hieroglyphics after the move are intended to indicate the comment "looks good, but is actually very bad!"

PLAY NOW CONTINUES:

	White	Black
8	Q–K2!	NxQBP ch
9	K–Q1	NxR
10	PxP dis ch	B–K2
11	PxP	

8 ... NxB, 9 PxP dis ch is no better.

9 ... N–Q5 would be answered by 10 Q–K4!, etc.

and it is all over.

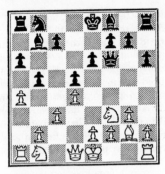

Position after 8 ... P-Q4?

The chess world was rather stunned when **Spassky** had the nerve to use 2 ... P-QN4!? in the 1966 world championship match, against **Petrosian.** Since then the line has become more and more popular, particularly as a suitable weapon for hacking out a win against the ultra-conservative 1 N-KB3 and 2 P-KN3. But paradoxically, it merely seems to increase White's chances of gaining the full point! In the diagrammed position we find Ghizdavu flexing his muscles far too early in the game, with the inevitable result . . .

THE OPENING MOVES WERE:

Keene	Ghizdavu
(Jerusalem, 1967)	
1 N-KB3	N-KB3
2 P-KN3	P-QN4!?

I myself have grown tired of throwing away countless points by trying to refute this type of play by White in the first 20 moves, and am now content merely to copy the enemy plan, at least until we both get safely castled. Not to be recommended theoretically perhaps—but very good statistically!

3 P-QB3!	

The idea is to rule out Black's normal "automatic" reply ... P-N5 when the inevitable P-QR4 is played.

The famous Petrosian-Spassky game mentioned above went: 3 P-QR4 P-N5, 4 P-Q3 B-N2, 5 P-K4 P-Q3, 6 B-N2 QN-Q2, 7 O-O P-K3, 8 P-R5? (this achieves nothing at all) R-QN1, 9 QN-Q2 B-K2, 10 N-QB4 O-O, 11 R-K1 P-QR3, 12 B-KB4 B-R1, with equality.

3 ...	B-N2
4 P-QR4	P-QR3
5 P-Q4	P-K3
6 B-KN5	P-KR3
7 BxN	QxB
8 B-N2	P-Q4?

PLAY NOW CONTINUED:

9 PxP	PxP
10 RxR	BxR
11 Q-N3!	

and Black has to leave the pawn en prise to deal with the threatened invasion of the White Queen via R2 and R7.

Position after 6 ... P–Q5?

Possibly the most extraordinary of all fianchetto openings is 1 P–KN4!?, a bizarre debut called the "Spike" which is the speciality of the Swiss player Grob. The Soviet grandmaster Keres has also ventured it in the occasional postal game, during his younger days. Anti-positional as it seems, the opening cannot be taken too lightly. The top diagrammed position shows a typical situation arising from premature pawn-grabbing by Black.

THE OPENING MOVES WERE:

	White	Black
1	P–KN4!?	P–Q4
2	B–N2	BxP!?
3	P–QB4!	P–QB3
4	Q–N3	Q–B2
5	PxP	PxP
6	N–QB3	P–Q5?

2 ... P–QB3, seems best.

With a concealed threat to White's QB.

Thinking that any Knight move to the fifth rank will block either the vital diagonal or the QN file.

PLAY NOW CONTINUES:

7	N–N5	Q–N3
8	BxP!	
8	...	B–K3
9	Q–KB3	QxN
10	BxR	

But the blocked QN file is to White's advantage!

8 ... QxB?? obviously loses the Queen.

and Black has no compensation for the exchange deficit.

Position after 6 . . . Q–B2?

An interesting counterattack available to Black at the third move is . . . N–KB3!?, although with best play White still retains the initiative. White's strongest line is 4 PxP NxP, 5 Q–N3! P–QB3 (5 . . . P–K3?? loses a piece after 6 Q–R4 ch), 6 QxP. Now Black *cannot* trap the White Queen in the corner with . . . Q–B2.

PLAY NOW CONTINUES:

7 QxR	N–N3
8 BxP ch!	B–Q2
9 Q–N7	

and the White Queen comes up smiling after all! (But 9 BxB ch?? would be a terrible blunder, because of . . . KxB!, threatening mate and the Queen.)

Readers who wish to know more about this fascinating opening should write to Grob at Postfach 248, Zurich 32, to purchase the 60-page analytical work *Grob's Angriff*.

Position after 9 B–KN5?

THE OPENING MOVES WERE:

The fifth game of the **Spassky-Larsen** match at Malmo, 1968, part of the elimination tournament for the 1969 world championship, featured some interesting play in the ancient Three Knights Opening. Spassky's 5 NxP against Black's fianchetto defence is considered somewhat inferior to 5 N–Q5!, and indeed this opinion was vindicated when Spassky eventually lost the game (his only defeat in the match, which he won overwhelmingly by 5½–2½). At the ninth move, a little-known variation of the thematic ... NxKP centre trap became a possibility.

	Spassky	Larsen
1	P–K4	P–K4
2	N–KB3	N–QB3
3	N–B3	P–KN3

This quaint line, a great favourite of Alekhine and more recently of Keres, is made playable by White's passive third move.

4	P–Q4	PxP
5	NxP	B–N2
6	B–K3	N–B3
7	B–K2	

Prameshuber-Keres, Munich, 1958, continued 7 B–QB4 O–O, 8 NxN NPxN, 9 P–K5 N–K1, 10 P–K6 BPxP, 11 BxP ch K–R1 with advantage to Black.

7	...	O–O
8	O–O	R–K1!

Setting two nasty traps, the first one being 9 P–B3? P–Q4!, with tremendous pressure in the centre. At this point (as one very often finds in master games of course) Spassky avoided the other pitfall involved, and played 9 NxN NPxN, 10 B–B3 B–QN2, 11 Q–Q2 P–Q3, 12 B–R6, and Larsen took the initiative with 12 ... BxB!, 13 QxB R–K4, winning on the 38th move. If he had tried the "obvious" pin instead, then ...

9 B–KN5?

PLAY WOULD THEN HAVE CONTINUED:

9	...	NxN
10	QxN	NxP!
11	QxN	RxQ
12	BxQ	BxN
13	PxB	RxB
14	KR–K1	RxR ch
15	RxR	P–QB3

and White cannot retrieve his pawn.

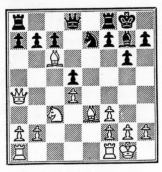

Position after 11 BxN?

One unorthodox way to bring pressure to bear on the White centre, in the Queen's Gambit, is to combine a King's side fianchetto with 2 ... N–QB3. This unusual theme occurred in the game **Fuster–Bronstein,** Budapest vs Moscow, 1949. The main drawback of Tschigorin's idea is that an early Q–QR4 by White is very difficult to parry, because Black's QB is absent from his post at B1, and the Black QNP is thereby rendered particularly vulnerable. But White must be careful to choose the right time to chase it, as the diagrammed position shows.

THE OPENING MOVES WERE:

	Fuster	Bronstein
1	P–Q4	P–Q4
2	P–QB4	N–QB3!?
3	N–KB3	

This move is designed to stop Black's latent threat ... P–K4 for all time. 3 N–QB3 also does the trick, but other attempts have proved less successful:

Unzicker–Barden, Hastings, 1950/51: 3 PxP QxP, 4 N–KB3 P–K4!, 5 N–B3 B–QN5, 6 B–Q2 BxN, 7 BxB P–K5 with equality.

Reti–Bogoljubov, Kiel, 1921: 3 P–K3? P–K4!, 4 PxKP P–Q5, 5 PxP QxP, 6 QxQ NxQ, 7 B–Q3 B–KN5, 8 P–B3 B–K3, 9 B–K3 O–O–O with advantage to Black.

3	...	B–N5
4	Q–R4	BxN
5	KPxB	P–K3
6	N–B3	KN–K2
7	B–K3	P–KN3
8	PxP	PxP
9	B–QN5?	

This pin seems inappropriate here. Perhaps Fuster had in mind his faulty 11th and 12th moves.

9	...	B–N2
10	O–O	O–O
11	BxN?	

Obviously intent on either chasing pawns with 12 Q–N5, or forcing Black to spoil his formation by 11 ... PxB.

PLAY NOW CONTINUED:

11 ... NxB, 12 Q–N5 NxP! (doubtless White thought this questionable in view of his Rook manoeuvre at the 14th turn), 13 BxN BxB, 14 QR–Q1 P–QB3!, 15 QxNP Q–N3, with very good prospects for the endgame.